A.720. RENOVATION

A.720. RENOVATION

Adding On

An Artful Guide to Affordable Residential Additions

Adding On

An Artful Guide to Affordable Residential Additions

Duo Dickinson

McGraw-Hill Book Company

New York   St. Louis   San Francisco   Auckland   Bogotá   Hamburg   Johannesburg
London   Madrid   Mexico   Montreal   New Delhi   Panama   Paris
São Paulo   Singapore   Sydney   Tokyo   Toronto

The McGraw-Hill Building Types Series

WATSON & LABS
Climatic Design (1982)

DICKINSON
Adding On: An Artful Guide to Affordable Residential Additions (1985)

DICKINSON
Small Houses: An Artful Guide to Affordable Residential Designs (1985)

BARR & BROUDY
Designing to Sell: The Art of Retail Store Design and Merchandising (1985)

BEDNAR
Planning and Building the New Atrium (1985)

DIBNER & DIBNER-DUNLAP
Building Additions Design Manual (1985)

HEPLER and WALLACH
The Home Planners' Guide to Residential Design (1986)

TARANATH
Structural Analysis and Design of Tall Buildings (1986)

LABS
Architecture Underground (1987)

Library of Congress Cataloging in Publication Data

Dickinson, Duo.
    Adding on.

    Includes index.
    1. Dwellings—Remodeling.   2. Architecture, Domestic.
I. Title.
TH4816.D53 1985   728   84-838
ISBN 0-07-016814-8

1 2 3 4 5 6 7 8 9 0 HAL/HAL 8 9 8 7 6 5 4

ISBN 0-07-016814-8

The editors for this book were Joan Zseleczky and Susan Killikelly, the designer was Duo Dickinson, and the production supervisor was Reiko F. Okamura. It was set in Auriga by Waldman Graphics.

Printed and bound by Halliday Lithograph.

We have tried to minimize so-called sexist language in this book. However, we have also tried to avoid such awkward constructions as "his/her" and "he/she," and the two objectives are not always compatible. Very rarely, we were forced to choose between an absurdly artificial expression and a more familiar masculine term. We opted for the latter, intending that the term be taken generically, to apply to both men and women.

For Liz

Contents

LIVING ROOMS AND FRONT DOORS

THE COMPLETE OVERHAUL

ARCHITECTS' AND DESIGNERS' DIRECTORY, 176

INDEX, 177

Foreword

Architecture is the choreography of the familiar and the surprising, and if a building doesn't have any of the familiar in it, people just can't relate to it at all. If it's zoomy future space or superhistoric neo-Georgian, there is no way of touching it. On the other hand, if it's altogether familiar, it doesn't interest anybody either, for there's no reason to bother with it.

If architects succeed, it is when they make something that is basically familiar but that has surprises in it, whether they mean to or not. It's like seasoning in food, which at best brings out the basic tastes that are there. Perhaps this is the manner in which an addition brings out the qualities in a house. The worst kinds of surprises in addition design are the ones that mask or desperately distort the familiar qualities that are there in the first place.

What I seem to see in myself (and I think it goes for most architects as they grow older) is that the familiar seems more and more important and the amount of surprise that is required diminishes.

A great many of the best-known architects in North America got their start doing little houses for their relatives or, even more often, doing famous additions to other people's houses. Normally, when they have grown somewhat older and acquired a more expensive office, they either have other work to do or can't afford to take on the tiny jobs with their tiny fees. So most additions are the early work of people, some of whom became well known later for much grander buildings. One of the difficulties with this is that the scope for the young architect doing additions is not nearly so grand as his desire to excel or, if you will, his ego. A young architect is likely to put all the things that are in his mind into any one job—"It might be the only job I ever get; I don't want to leave out anything." In this case, the amount of what's new in the design is likely to be fairly large and the amount of what's familiar in it may be quite small or even too little. That's why people are always talking about "weird architects," almost always "weird young architects" (except in a few cases of arrested development), who have done some wild things they find interesting but can't relate to very well.

I think if you've done a body of work or just naturally simmered down, it might seem you have fewer ideas, or maybe I'd like to think you just get a more relaxed notion of how much more new you need in a job to spice it up and how much of the familiar you need to make people feel comfortable with it.

What is so apparent in the additions shown in this book, and in any small architectural project, is that it isn't the architect's unbounded ego but the client's ego that's at stake; that's why the client is doing it. In addition to wanting to have hot water in the pipes, the client wants to have something that expresses himself, that is an extension of himself and not an extension of some architect that he just met.

The architect fresh from training in school has had no background of being sensitive to the problems of somebody else's ego. The student has had no background at all in changing things, for he is trained in school to come up with something to be criticized for, and that's the end of it.

The main process in doing anything from an addition on forward or backward is cutting and fitting, trying something and seeing what goes and what doesn't go, and then gracefully and usefully changing the notion to fit the images that are in the client's head.

The client is not trained to express and to describe what he wants and just cannot write a program that gives a foolproof outline for making the right shapes and right space and right light coming in at the right time. I remember a woman for whom I did a house who appeared at one of the meetings at which we were presenting little cardboard models. She brought with her a huge kitchen knife and started stabbing holes in the walls where she wanted windows!

The danger in client input lies in the willingness to move parts of the house as if they were pieces of furniture. Moving furniture is not too horrible a way of expressing yourself in a house that doesn't fit you, because it doesn't cost too much and it is a way of laying on hands, trying to make the place your own.

One of the first questions an architect should ask the client with an addition or remodel is, "Are you really making this house do more better, or are you just moving around the parts at considerable expense to no special purpose?" The real answer is too often the latter.

In the period when my firm was doing mostly houses, I calculated that the average number of complete changes in the kitchen plan, in the hands of the person in charge of the kitchen, was twenty-six. These changes have expensive consequences.

For me the most interesting thing is to figure out how adding something can change everything. The whole notion of remodel is that with one new piece, the emphases, the rhythms, and the qualities of light and space in the whole house become all new. What does not interest me very much is the addition that just leaves your old house behind, forgets it, and builds a new piece of architecture as though it were out in the middle of a prairie.

A great many architects have done additions that have rather cavalierly cast aside the house to which they are adding in order to make something that would cause the world to sit up and take notice. These additions themselves are often very exciting, but they leave you wishing the old house would go away.

The excellence of additions, and one of the special qualities of the additions in this book, is that they don't cast aside the houses that they are a part of, but manage to do the things they do and make the experience of the houses more exciting, more interesting, more of an extension of the people who live in them. The ancients would have called it magic.

Certainly, part of the problem of our time is that we are the heirs of the 1950s, which are often cast as the villain these days. That decade had an attitude somewhere between embarrassment and hate toward existing buildings. So a perfectly standard remodeling of the 1940s, 1950s, or 1960s would yank off the loathed ornament and Band-Aid it over with whatever piece of plywood or Masonite was handy.

I think there are all sorts of qualities of existing houses that are familiar and become important, such as dignity. It is really very strange and not very satisfying to see a perfectly dignified house get tarted up like a middle-aged lady in a disco outfit. With age comes a set of qualities, and dignity is one of the nicer ones.

I sometimes wonder with terror what people are going to think of our remodelings, whether they will seem like enhancements or flat-out disfigurements.

Among the qualities of the American dream that have made a mysterious disappearance over the years since World War II are those clustered around thrift, economy, the maximum of means, all achieved with Yankee ingenuity. I'm fond of saying about a great many student designs, the work of colleagues, and even sometimes my own, that "the work would benefit from a 25 percent cut in the budget." One of the excellences of this book is that it revives the pleasures of those astringent virtues like economy as it shows additions that have greatly changed the mood and sense of excitement of existing houses, even more importantly than they have added to their accommodations. The best examples of these add-ons have made a whole new world mostly, and very efficiently, out of existing parts. In this book the designs are assembled (and they were assembled very carefully after a great number were examined) because they do accomplish something. They make interesting, even occasionally inspirational, reading.

—Charles W. Moore

Introduction

A SHIFTING CONTEXT

Along with Mom and apple pie, the single-family house is one of the few absolute American priorities. With discouragingly high interest rates and the exorbitant cost of new construction, families who are seeking their first home or who have outgrown their present accommodations are finding themselves caught in a financial and spatial squeeze. Cooperatives, condominiums, government-subsidized mortgages, and owner financing have provided a certain measure of stopgap accommodation. But for those who do not have these alternatives, what is the solution to finding a home that is both affordable and functionally viable?

It is my contention that rather than give up a home purchased with "cheap" money to build anew with more expensive funding, the American home owner will opt to modify and rejuvenate what is in hand. Rather than make do in a pint-sized co-op or condo or flush money down the drain of rental, those seeking a first home will find a viable alternative to new construction in the plethora of inexpensive existing homes that show enough potential to encourage investment in some thoughtful work.

The emergence of the addition as a standard solution rather than a makeshift option for the American home owner has its origins in unique demographic and aesthetic circumstances. After the two world wars, doughboys and GIs came home to sweethearts and ripe economies, creating immediate residential building booms. The automobile and cheap gas facilitated an exurban sprawl on the outskirts of every urban center in the United States. The last thirty years have seen the flight of business headquarters to the promised land of country club living, corporate campuses, and alluring tax benefits—further spreading the congestion of suburban America. Sites have dried up, property values have skyrocketed, and the houses built to turn a profit generations ago are now showing their age. Many major urban areas in America are feeling the pinch, especially Washington, D.C., the suburbs of New York, Los Angeles, Denver, the cities of the Sunbelt, as well as small-town New England.

Concurrent with these social migrations, the Arab oil embargo of 1975 forever changed America's criteria for desirable residential architecture. If a building does not address the need to conserve energy and mitigate absurd heating and cooling costs, it is judged defective. Whereas it was once an optional feature, energy efficiency is now a bottom-line criterion for the desirability of a home design. This emphasis can be seen in the growing number of architect-designed additions with passive solar intentions, supplanting the quick fix of a prefab greenhouse or sun-space tack-on. Travel distances have become so significant in terms of fuel costs that an influx of upper-middle-class refugees from suburbia is rediscovering the joys of urban living. Otherwise known as gentrification, this migration threatens traditional neighborhoods thoughout our urban centers.

Concurrent with these social and economic movements, several recent aesthetic currents have helped engender a renewed respect for existing buildings and have caused architects to reconsider the option of reworking existing structures in lieu of constructing completely new houses.

During the excess of urban-renewal demolition in the 1950s and 1960s, a core of committed citizens began the Historic Preservation movement, which has now been graduated as a fully functional in-place bureaucracy with laws and regulations set up to foster the retrieval of buildings threatened by man or nature (or both).

Perhaps the best-documented movement of recent building design has been the so-called Post-Modernist movement, whose traditional or historical motifs are caricatured in playful postures in new construction. This trendy bandwagon lends acceptance toward the homely aesthetics contemporary architecture has spent the better part of this century rejecting.

As a corollary to both the Historic Preservation and Post-Modernist movements, a renewed sensitivity by architects to a building's surrounding neighborhood has been dubbed Contextualism by those who label aesthetic intentions. Quite simply, Contextualism urges a sympathetic response to existing conditions where once architects felt compelled to heroically reject a building's context.

These three movements, implicitly or directly linked, have to a greater or lesser extent helped contemporary architects undergo the aesthetic equivalent of sensitivity training regarding the existing buildings around them.

The last decade encompassing these aesthetic evolutions has seen the availability of money, land, and energy dry up. As these shortages are combined with a huge pressurization of the market as the baby-boom babies have babies, I believe we are on the advent of a discovery that the addition can mean infinitely more than simply added space.

THE STATE OF THE ART—
PERCEIVED AND EXISTING

There are literally millions upon millions of American homes no longer functionally or economically viable. The inhabitants of these buildings, American middle-class families, have been ill-served by the thoughtless agglomeration of space that has defined the typical residential addition.

The problem is a failure of imagination, and applied imagination is the architect's method of survival.

Common public perception of residential addition design is prejudiced by the way these projects have traditionally been conceived. The typically expedient addition has all the charm and appeal of an idiot cousin. In response to a functional evolution (children, new kitchen, or videocassette recorder), houses seem to spring gratuitous cancers accommodating the new activities with the subtle sensibility of a lean-to tent.

Who "designed" these growths? Often it was the builder who knew what would stand up but valued the bottom line as the arbiter of his aesthetic, or the decorator who photocopied whatever magazine article struck a fancy—structure, environment, and leaks be damned. Or perhaps it was the owners themselves who with the full building ignorance of the decorator and the stylistic incompetence of the builder sallied forth with the innocent enthusiasm of soldiers hitting a beachhead. The resulting additions are often quite sad in appearance and utility and are frequently removed within a generation or two.

Sensitive and innovative additions *do* exist. A small percentage of the work is done by architects in the proto-

professional stages of their careers or during times of economic recession or depression. But because of the predominant image of the typically expedient addition, the field of serious architectural criticism has shied away from this body of work.

Unfortunately, if the architect is to become a viable choice to answer the needs of the average home owner, he must deal with a negative public perception. He must fight the twin myths of the Howard Roarkian ego that sweeps aside the needs of a client, and the architect-designed project as an open financial floodgate of unrestrained cost. This can be done by the exposure of the thoughtful work that is going on today. The examples shown in this book hopefully display a sensitivity and responsiveness that do not compromise creativity. Success in design is not merely the cheap thrill of a heroic statement. Without a depth of understanding of an existing building's properties and a client's needs, the addition can be a sorry joke.

The bulk of the homes in America turn a deaf ear toward their owners and deserve only a passing paean to the ingenuity of capitalism in pumping out just enough amenity to facilitate a healthy profit. The average home-desiring family is stuck in the "something is better than nothing" consciousness of mass production affordability—unless creativity is given a free hand. Since the home is the last best hope of our egos and our wallets, I cannot believe that we will settle for the standard when the exceptional is shown to be possible. America has the largest blank canvas of buildings in the world and a huge market desiring the space, economies, and visceral thrill so starkly absent from these boxes. There are architects creating, out of necessity, a mountain of work out of many little molehills.

These photos represent a walk down memory lane. We have all seen an undesigned addition or perhaps been actively involved in the process of building one. Although planned and carefully considered by the home owner, the generic addition does not have many ambitions beyond simple spatial expansion in a convenient manner.

This montage is not intended to mock or point a finger in anger. The projects shown are archetypes of what has been the norm for residential additions in America. Usually laid out by the owners or builders without training in or awareness of the rules implicit in the existing buildings, these projects are rarely ugly but seldom beautiful, with their impact to the interested observer usually ranging from slightly awkward to cheerfully ad hoc.

Each of these projects is a bit of living history for the family involved and represents a level of success and confidence that allows for the laying on of hands.

Photos by Sue Ann Miller

THE DIFFERENCES WITH ADDITIONS

In order to better understand and evaluate the examples in this book, it is a good idea to address the specialized methods and criteria used to effect the solutions shown. Despite the best efforts of morphological analysis and academic methodology, the design process remains an ambiguous, highly personal phenomenon.

However, unless the complexities inherent in deriving a transformative addition solution are outlined, the examples shown lose their full meaning. It is not enough to apprehend the physical content of the addition, for in its own unique way the addition best manifests the dynamic interface between the family and the home that both nurtures the growth and reflects the character of its occupants.

In designing a new home, the architect proposes (with seductive presentations and visionary musings) and the client disposes (with his checkbook). In the addition project, it is often the client who proposes, since years of occupancy can create a familiarity with the existing building that no architect could hope to have. In response, the architect must take the specific truths of his client's knowledge and infuse his scheme with a utility only guessed at in new construction design. It is the twin bases of the family and the existing building that mesh with an architect's vision to create a result both inspirationally new and reassuringly rooted in the original building. Such rich results come only with an intense analysis of the existing conditions and the family's needs. Given the aforementioned depth of programmatic input and the importance of an architect's familiarity with existing construction techniques plus his ability to effect his desires in new construction, an addition project tests an architect's talent and training more than the standard new building project. The very acts of cataloging and depicting an existing building, involving site inspection and field measurement, can be quite intimidating to most architects.

Architects are seemingly called upon to have X-ray vision to see existing utility systems, structural decay, or existing load-bearing capacity within a sealed building envelope. Understandably, an architect's instincts and experience can often prove frustratingly inadequate. The liabilities are often great. This is why many builders as well as architects have shied away from undertaking addition work. However, because of the enormous needs described earlier and the depressed state of the design profession, more and more architects are willing to take on the risks and express themselves via the addition.

In an addition project, an architect must synthesize the intricacies of both the programmatic input of the clients and the condition of the existing structure as evidenced in the building. To help the reader better understand the complex basis upon which an addition design is undertaken, it is appropriate to outline those areas that must be addressed by the architect. The following checklist is not intended to be complete, rather it can serve as a fundamental listing of those issues that make an addition a unique design problem.

I Codes and regulations
A. Read all applicable zoning ordinances and check the following:
   1) Setback requirements.
   2) Height limitations.
   3) Existing type of zoning in place for the site.
   4) The procedure for variance or special-exception application. Bear in mind all probable time needed for such procedures during the preliminary design and scheduling of the project.
B. Determine whether the site is in a Historic District, wetlands-management and coastal flood-plain area, or any other location subject to extraordinary regulations.
C. If the building is not up to code minimums and the violations, while not affecting life safety, would bankrupt the project budget, speak to the building inspector or consult the local code to determine exactly what percentage of capital improvement

(30 to 40 percent of the building's assessed value, typically) constitutes a major renovation in the eyes of the code, causing the entire structure to be liable for a complete review of code compliance by the local building inspector. This can be disastrous to the owner's capability to afford the addition.

II Inspection of the existing building and integration of the addition

A. Foundation
   1) Check for water damage present and past.
   2) Determine what new subsoil drainage must be added.
   3) Determine whether existing settlement indicates an unfortunate subsoil condition invisible from the outside.
   4) In designing the new addition, make sure to do the following adequately:
      a) Regrade earth around the addition's perimeter to drain water away from the building.
      b) Overlap new and old waterproofing membranes.
      c) Integrate new foundations with old to prevent uneven settling.

B. Structural conditions
   1) Determine the existing framing structure.
      a) Carefully sketch the plan while on site.
      b) Inspect the basement and attic.
      c) If all else fails, assume the short-span-is-best theory; that is, in oblong rooms the longer set of parallel walls are load-bearing.
   2) Inspect for deformation by looking for the following:
      a) Surface cracks on finish surfaces.
      b) Moldings popped away from existing position.
      c) Door and window frames that are out of square; notice whether the trim miters are tight or coming apart.
      d) Excessive vibration when you jump up and down.
   3) Determine if the deformation is recent by finding out the last time the evidence above was repaired. If the home is out of square but there is no recent movement, then the structure has probably stabilized, allowing for a safe addition.

C. Mechanical systems
   1) Locate plumbing stacks and utility chases via basement and attic inspection.
   2) Determine the existing state of heating-plant and insulation efficiency. If there are inadequacies, the addition can and should rectify the problems as much as possible.
   3) Unless absolutely necessary do not move the following:
      a) Utility chases.
      b) Plumbing stacks.
      c) Water and utility lines.
      d) Septic systems.
   4) Always consult a professional contractor or engineer about the adequacy of various systems' capacities and indicate their recommendations in the bidding and construction documents.

D. Exterior membrane
   1) Inspect for leaks.
   2) Determine if flashing or ventilation is adequate to prevent rot.
   3) Avoid exterior concave corners when adding on.
   4) In the design of the addition, extend existing planes where possible (roof, wall, etc.). Do not try to weave surfaces older than five or ten years with new material; resurface where continuity is desired.
   5) Reuse existing openings where possible.

III Interior indications of existing occupant needs

A. Use patterns
   1) Inadequate spaces tend to have the following:
      a) Too many functions occurring within them.
      b) Essential furnishings only, few amenities.
      c) Signs of heavy use, i.e., wear, dirt, etc.
   2) Underutilized spaces have the following:
      a) Dust and lint versus tracked-in dirt or handprints on walls.
      b) Furniture legs furrowed into carpets, indicating long-term static positioning.
   3) Since it is always cheaper to alter internally rather then add externally, combine inadequate and underutilized spaces wherever possible.

B. Circulation
   1) Determine existing circulation patterns.
      a) Walk the various sequences of the house.
      b) Sketch the plan carefully while on the site.
      c) Look for carpet wear and wall soiling.
      d) Determine which exterior doors are used the most.
   2) Do not move stairs unless absolutely necessary; consider the existing stairs as the endpoints of a desirable circulation pattern.
   3) If necessary, do not hesitate to revise existing patterns to do the following:
      a) Clarify entry vista.
      b) Minimize space occupied by the circulation path.
      c) Minimize changes in direction.

The gist of this is quite simple: Be thorough in the evaluation of the existing conditions and be cautious about the assumptions you make.

The architect must strive to *reduce* the area of the new part of the building to be added on. If that can be accomplished by rerouting circulation for maximum efficiency or by combining underutilized spaces with inadequate spaces, large amounts of money can be saved or reallocated for the amenities and features that can enrich even the most brilliant solution.

Thoroughness and caution at the outset of the project can facilitate seemingly effortless and eloquent solutions to complex problems.

CONTRACTS AND RELATIONSHIPS: A SPECIAL NOTE

The addition project is a team effort. Because there is a building to react to, clients have a depth of input and a personal investment much greater than in a project involving only new construction. Since the builder is operating in an existing home, his role in the project impacts on the clients far more directly than in new construction, where he is seldom observed and never intrudes on the clients' day-to-day life. It is the architect who bears the burden of dealing with both the clients' legitimate fears and the builder's awkward position of house wrecker. Because of these complex and intimate interrelationships, it is fitting that prior to the description of so many faits accomplis the human components' essential roles are outlined.

1. The Clients

The family desiring to modify their built environment should be prepared for an enormous disruption of their daily lives. They should also be prepared to deal with complex decisions that have permanent implications for their lives while living in their renovated house. Hence all family members should do their homework and prepare a list of all areas of concern and need, down to the most mundane issues. An architect is not a mind reader, and what elements clients do not advocate, they may end up regretting the absence of later.

With the exigencies of addition projects well documented, the client should set aside a 10 to 15 percent contingency fund above and beyond the actual agreed-upon bid figure for those areas no one could possibly foresee given the physical evidence at hand. Patience, goodwill, and a sense of humor are often as important as money in making the act of architectural revision an exciting, positive experience.

2. The Architect

The architect should realize that he will be under closer scrutiny from clients when designing an addition than when designing new construction. The clients' familiarity with the existing home can be a tool that can be used in generating a scheme, or it can be a barrier to a project's execution when an architect's vision ignores the clients' specific input.

The costs of addition-renovation construction, as said, are much harder to predict, hence an intermediate solicitation for nonbinding budget bids from builders at an early design phase is very useful to nail down the real costs involved. A secondary benefit is in the input gained from builders' reactions to the design presented. Often one feature will represent an enormously inflated cost relative to its functional or aesthetic importance and can be changed prior to final bidding.

The architect should be prepared to be flexible. Once a wall or two is moved, the architect, or the builder, or the client may have an entirely new reaction to the design, and the scheme should best respond to take advantage of the potentials exposed. The architect serves as the anchor of faith for clients during a time of extreme anxiety—major surgery on a dear old friend. In his ability to listen to a builder's input, he can generate a sense of working together versus creating an adversary relationship that is poisonous to an addition project, where professional responsibilities can be ambiguous.

It is best for an architect to let the clients determine his fee in an addition project—via a fixed percentage of the building's cost serving as the method of fee determination. The more that is desired by the clients, generally the more the architect must labor to effect the final design, hence, the more he should be compensated.

3. The Builder

Additions are unlike all other building projects. As previously mentioned, they require more patience, knowledge, and planning than new constructions. Consequently, they cost more per square foot than new construction. Given these problems, some builders will not bid competitively on these projects, so the best method for getting a good list of contractors to send drawings to for bid purposes is by personal referral. This is especially true in addition work, since the builder's contact with the clients is both intimate and highly pressurized. In reworking an existing home, a builder both disrupts a family's lifestyle and physically abuses a very dear possession. Cleanliness, manners, and style are more important than a high level of skill in terms of getting the project built with a minimum of pain and anxiety.

Accurate bids depend on a complete set of drawings and specifications and a thorough site inspection with the architect present. Since the unknowns in dealing with an existing building create enormous contractual ambiguities, the completeness of drawings and specs by the architect is crucial to get an accurate bid back from the builder. Occasionally, a builder will be unwilling to fix a price on some aspect of the construction he cannot be sure of—the full extent of existing rot to be repaired, for example—and the clients and the architect must either have the confidence to trust his honest accounting of the work done or opt for a builder who is willing to assume a price. More often than not in such cases, a fixed price is greatly inflated beyond the actual costs of time and materials, since the builder must protect himself unless he needs work more than he needs a guaranteed profit.

These interrelationships can blossom with trust or become disastrous when suspicions are raised. All parts of the equation must realize that the scheduling, costs, and designs are more flexible and variable in an addition project due to the basic uncertainties of dealing with existing buildings that in some cases are centuries old. If the personalities involved are similarly responsive and sensitive, the addition is perhaps the most educational and rewarding of all building projects.

Otto Baitz

Mark McInturff

Arne Bystrom

Steve Badanes

Robert Perron

Kimo Griggs

Jim Adamson

H. Durston Saylor

Mark McInturff

Mark Mc...

Robert Perron

Fred Leavitt

KITCHENS AND BACK DOORS

Often including the mudroom, laundry, informal dining area, and family room, the kitchen space has become the hearth of contemporary America.

INTRODUCTION

The standard builder's home constructed in the 1920s or 1950s tended to put spatial and budgetary emphasis on the more formal parts of the house: the living room, the dining room, and the foyer. Consequently, the other spaces relegated to the first floor, the kitchen and informal entry, were shortchanged. The typical farmhouse has often had its country kitchen pared down in subsequent remodeling, frequently to create a formal dining area. In the average Victorian home, the kitchen was designed as one of several small rooms placed out of sight, perhaps with a back door. In short, most of the existing American homes designed prior to 1970 have placed a limited importance on creating functionally versatile or architecturally sumptuous kitchens.

Because of the lightening of rigid social customs and the impossibility of finding affordable domestic help in the 1980s, the kitchen has evolved into a hub of both familial and social congregations. Until a decade or two ago, servants would disappear into a stark kitchen of sink, range, and refrigerator to emerge magically several hours later with multicourse meals served on platters and in tureens. Today, any family member old enough to press a microwave's "on" button and pop open a toaster oven can feed a family of five in half an hour.

With the disappearance of servants and the proliferation of labor-saving devices, the kitchen has become the setting for the social and dramatic act of modern food preparation. With the volatility of food prices, storage space is now as desirable as it was in an era of less-then-easy transportation. The net result is a kitchen whose physical requirements have become more complex and space-consuming.

The piggyback to this late-twentieth-century an informal living area in close proximity to, or more usually as part of, the space in which the kitchen resides. This informal area is otherwise known as the family room, breakfast nook, or informal dining area.

The changing nature of contemporary kitchen use is a social phenomenon. The kitchen is no longer a "black box" emitting a finished product; as an informal living area it is used to feed the family, accommodate dinner guests, and display the home owner's latest High Tech appliances.

Subsequently the home owner does not need merely a "new look" for his or her old kitchen. A cosmetic resurfacing is woefully inadequate to address the new needs stated; hence the architect can be employed to bring generalist knowledge to bear on the gross inadequacies of the traditional American kitchen.

Another function pivoting from the kitchen is the mudroom and back door entry, often in the form of an air lock to reduce air filtration. Frequently the laundry area is moved into close proximity with said mudroom for obvious reasons. When the half bath is not present or is located in an awkard position in the existing house, it is often subtly inserted near the rear entry.

The functional evolution of the informal areas of the American home has been rooted in the emergence of the kitchen as the acknowledged social center of the family. Where once families huddled in cramped quarters dodging the culinary shrapnel implicit in food preparation, the need for expansion has finally begun to be overtly expressed in additions throughout all areas of the country in all income groups.

Going Up!

Louis Mackall piggybacks onto an existing addition to decongest a home in Greenwich, Connecticut.

In overpriced Greenwich, Connecticut, a modest home on a quarter-acre lot costs more than most custom-built homes on spacious situations elsewhere. Peter and Syd Uhry were gravely aware of that fact when they opted to buy their modest home so near and yet so far from New York City. The key to their purchase was the extraordinary view to the south for such an ordinary home in Greenwich; a brook and pond created a delightful park at the end of their street, giving the Uhrys a shared but thoroughly appreciated backyard.

The only problem was that this single expansive feature was invisible from inside the house. Given the nature of a young family's finances, discontent with amenity had to await both functional necessity and financial feasibility.

Once their two children outgrew tiny rooms, the Uhrys decided it was time to act. However, they soon learned that a traditional horizontal expansion of the building's mass proved impossible given the fact the house had already occupied the entire buildable portion of their lot according to ordinances governing the coastal area wetlands.

Beyond the simple need for more space, the kitchen and family room were wedged into an existing addition to the west of the house. The interior of this wing was an ad hoc disaster of pressed wallboard and oblique circulation patterns. In desperation, the Uhrys turned to Louis Mackall, an architect who tends to see the potentials in problems.

With children, view, kitchen, and yes, even bathrooms all pressing against the preemptive zoning regulations, Louis Mackall opted to gut the awkward kitchen wing and build a second story above it while doing

selective surgical insertion of new spaces in the existing house.

An informal kitchen-dining-living space took over the first floor of the gutted addition, and a celestial master bedroom rose above the kitchen, allowing one child to take over the old master bedroom. Additionally, two baths were created where there once was one, and an existing attic became a reading nook. Since the kitchen and family room area created is almost prototypical of the "new" kitchen, that space is the primary focus of the photos shown.

With so little space and so much to accommodate, Mackall used several devices to relieve the congestion. The new kitchen was kept as compact as possible using floor-to-ceiling storage along the north wall and a tight galley arrangement. This condensation allowed the informal living area to coexist in the same space, thus both areas benefit from the combined visual area.

An important aside greatly influenced the final result. Louis Mackall is also a principal in Breakfast Woodworks, a small, highly creative millwork house, and it was only because of his ability to reinvent standard cabinet detailing that so much functional activity could be distilled in such an efficient package.

All exterior detailing was made consistent with the existing house, allowing a restful shell to house some exciting spaces.

The brilliance of this scheme lies not in dramatic architecture but rather in subtle elegance derived from perfect functional fit and ingenious adaptation to limitations. The detailing is both invigorating and compatible with the existing conditions. So much can be done with so little if the opportunities can be allowed to flourish amid adversity.

PROJECT PROFILE

Uhry residence
Location: Greenwich, Conn.
Architect: Louis Mackall,
Louis Mackall & Partner
Budget: $60,000*
Area renovated: 400 ft^2
Area added: 350 ft^2

*Unless otherwise specified, all dollar values are valid for the early 1980s.

OWNERS' STATEMENT

Sorting out our options, we decided to modify our living arrangement, or move. Although technically our house was a three-bedroom, two-bath, two-story Colonial, all our rooms were small. There was only one bathroom upstairs, with four of us using it. The kitchen was narrow and dark and held a hodgepodge of old cupboards. The southern view of a garden and pond were cut off by a bathroom and a closet.

Planning took five months, and construction seven. By vaulting some ceilings, placing the majority of new windows to the south, and using a liberal number of skylights, we gave our remodeled house a feeling of openness and light.—*Peter and Syd Uhry*

ARCHITECT'S STATEMENT

The Uhry addition and alteration were made up of several parts. In order of importance they are the kitchen-family room, master bedroom and bath, south terrace, and attic room. Of these, by far the most effort went into the first, for the space was tight and the demands on that space considerable. The key was arranging functions so that as little space as possible was taken up by circulation despite the fact that the main entrance to the house traveled right through the kitchen.

As I think about the job as a whole, there was a constant overlapping of usually separate functions. The pay dirt of our time is uncovering the relationships between things, discovering, and then bringing attention to, the ways they mutually complement each other. This is true at every level, from the overall plan for an addition and alteration down to the smallest details.—*Louis Mackall*

1

fig. 1 *Galley kitchen. Quarry-tile flooring only exists in the high-use area between counters, and a standard casement window is flanked by two custom fixed pane windows to create a small bay window, responding to the thrust of the galley's axis. A custom copper hood helps keep the space open and houses integral lighting fixtures.*

fig. 2 *Under construction. One can easily see the direct vertical extension of the existing floor and the new glazing facing south that captures light and view.*

2

3

4

fig. 3 *Family area. Southern glazing captures passive gain in winter and is shaded by exterior trellis during summer. Bookcase storage over seating area utilizes dead space to the maximum amount. Note 4-inch bull-nose molding above window and across bookcase. This element can be seen in the galley view as well and integrates the two spaces with a barely noticeable formal element.*

fig. 4 *Kitchen, north wall. Floor-to-ceiling storage is allowed to achieve maximum depth by recessing upper cabinets only as needed over counters. A system of beech frames and sandblasted glass fronts is used for all doors and drawers. Work surfaces and back splashes are glazed tile with a quarter-round beech counter edge, and eating surfaces are beech with purple-heart inlay. All wood is treated with urethane.*

5

6

7

8

fig. 5   *Master bath. Extended ceilings and shallow vanity enable a narrow bath to feel spacious. By utilizing a pedestal sink, Mackall allows for a generous basin while expressing the form of the ceramic mass in the custom cabinet. Counters are teak, frames are urethane-treated beech, shower wall and fronts are of sandblasted glass, and the medicine cabinet is inserted in the vertical fixed mirror.*

fig. 6   *Trellis. Facing south, this custom cedar trellis traps space and shades the view-catching new windows in the family room. Mackall reused a column owned by the Uhrys for support.*

fig. 7   *Master bedroom. Vaulted ceiling is punctuated by an asymmetrically placed round window.*

fig. 8   *Reading loft. Carved into existing attic space, this loft is a hideaway for adolescent daughters, who would otherwise be cramped by the small existing bedrooms.*

Photos by Joan Sussman

Beaming with Pride

Eric K. Rekdahl changes the focus of a kitchen using explicit structure and surface treatment.

PROJECT PROFILE

Riemann residence
Location: Kensington, Calif.
Architect: Eric K. Rekdahl,
Rekdahl Tellefsen Associates
Budget: $40,000
Area renovated: 284 ft^2
Area added: 57 ft^2

When dealing with an ill-conceived or deteriorated house, an architect can justify a great many revisions. But in the case of Dick and Renie Riemann's home in Kensington, California, the house was neither ugly nor endangered. The house in question was designed by John Hudson Thomas in 1928 in an Arts and Crafts Movement variation of Tudor. The house was beautiful, the site shielded from the street yet open to the woods, with a lovely southern exposure.

Unfortunately, the fly in the soup was the kitchen. Its total area was less than 120 square feet, and its lone window faced a dim north vantage. A serpentine circulation pattern caused anyone entering from the outside or ancillary spaces to invade and disrupt an already inadequate space.

Including and adjacent to the existing kitchen, there were six separate spaces in only 284 square feet of floor space, but designer Eric Rekdahl could see beyond the many walls and envision a new space that could embrace the multiple functions of the 1980s eat-in kitchen. However, even with all walls removed, the space was still a tad small. Fortunately, an existing entry porch provided the extra 57 square feet needed to accommodate a table for four.

Given the gut-and-conquer approach, an average designer might just plug in the standard construction methods of dimensional lumber and gypsum-wallboard skin to gloss over the minor inconsistencies, but Eric Rekdahl opted to use the existing structural technique as an integrating feature of his newfound space.

Two major beams were needed to collect

OWNER'S STATEMENT

Renie and I had numerous reasons for renovating the kitchen at our beloved Robins Wold (essentially in this order of importance):
- To gain physical elbow room. The main part of the old kitchen was a dark stop along a labyrinthine jungle path.
- To gain psychological space. The old kitchen confined one spiritually as well as physically.
- To make the kitchen stylistically integral to the house.

The new kitchen has become the heart(h) of our home and family life. Far more than food preparation now takes place in it. It also functions as Renie's planning space (desk) and Katie's play space (play stove and corner), while I am in touch through an open door to my work bench and desk in the garage. Guests can also now be entertained while meals are prepared, and we can eat our meals in the same room they're prepared in!—*Dick Riemann*

DESIGNER'S STATEMENT

The goal throughout the entire design-building process was to create a modern, functioning kitchen and eating area in harmony with Thomas's storybook English cottage. The remodeling should not be apparent at first glance. One should have to look for the modern conveniences to confirm one's suspicions. The architectural envelope should not give it away.

John Hudson Thomas created a fantasy of another era so strongly in this house that I felt compelled to learn his vocabulary of elements and to exploit them to evoke the same feelings in others that his details evoked in me.—*Eric K. Rekdahl*

the load once handled by interior and exterior walls now removed by the architect. Rekdahl picked up on the existing framing plan of the adjacent dining room and continued the spacing into the new kitchen area. Careful fluting of the beam edges and integral corner brackets mimicked existing conditions. By continuing the existing framing plan over the informal dining area only, Rekdahl allowed for an obvious break in ceiling height with the food-preparation area.

With care similar to that taken with the framing, Rekdahl succeeded in adapting existing muntin detailing to the custom glazing enclosing the onetime entry porch. Fortunately this new porch faced south, allowing for some passive solar gain. To maximize the heat retained and visually unify the new space, quarry tile was used as the new flooring material.

The kitchen cabinets were conceived as a simple echoing of the fir framing in tone and explicit joinery. They provide a consistent context, making the inserted (and obviously modern) appliances subtle events. Hollow clay tiles for the walls also blend with existing conditions. In a cooperative, hands-on spirit, Rekdahl served as contractor and beam fabricator on this project, and the clients salvaged the marble for their countertops as well.

It is easy to forget that pride and care have obvious consequences. In a world where expediency and the quick thrill are all too important, the Riemanns and Eric Rekdahl have displayed that a simple solution need not be simplistically expressed.

1   *Andy Whipple*

fig. 1 *Eating area, to the south. Note the seemingly frameless fixed glazing and the delicate muntin pattern. The fluting of the beam edge was done by the architect and is echoed in the table frame detailing.*

fig. 2 *Plans. A host of interior walls (dotted lines) were eliminated to straighten the circulation pattern and create a spacious kitchen. The existing porch was enclosed to accommodate dining.*

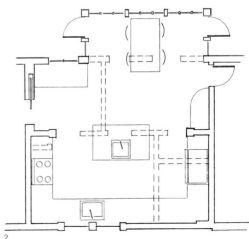

2

3

Andy Whipple

4

5

Eric K. Rekdahl

fig. 3 *Kitchen, facing north. The quietly expressive joinery of the cabinet fronts serves to create a consistent basis for the necessary intrusion of the appliances. Porcelain pulls serve as counterpoint to the wood.*

fig. 4 *Beam joinery. The expressed dowels, decorative carved fluting, and notched brackets convey a subtle animation of detailing seldom seen in contemporary design.*

fig. 5 *Exterior view. Nestled under an Arts and Crafts Movement gable end, the reclaimed porch blends well with its context.*

Contemporary Cascade

Shope Reno Wharton Associates use familiar materials to spring a lyrical statement from a prosaic house.

PROJECT PROFILE

Rodrigues residence
Location: Greenwich, Conn.
Architects: Shope Reno Wharton Associates
Budget: $40,000
Area renovated: 350 ft²
Area added: 250 ft²

Situated at the crest of a hill, Christopher and Priscilla Rodrigues's Colonial home lacked adequate space for two essential suburban activities, eating and parking.

Typical of a 1920s Colonial-style home, the kitchen was a backwater space of impossibly cramped dimensions. With the need to embrace cooking as part of their entertaining, the Rodriques family approached the young firm of Shope Reno Wharton about making their home more livable.

Beyond the simple needs of function and space, the architects soon realized that the sloping site provided ample opportunity to reach out to the view while providing access for a much-needed second garage space.

Given the boxlike mass of the existing house, adding anything to its simplistic shape was potentially awkward. A standard Colonial paste-on wing would look a bit silly flying into the void of the ravine. So with the owners' blessing, the architects endeavored to create a controlled kinetic massing, obviously springing from the house but reaching openly to the backyard.

The risk of being mockingly modern was avoided by basing the vertical dimensions of the various wall elements of the addition on the existing clapboard spacing module and wrapping that skin over the entire exposed surface. What results is the introduction of curving and angular geometries

OWNERS' STATEMENT

When we purchased this property, we realized that while it was in sound condition, the house needed some work in order for it to be an entirely satisfactory and livable space. Our criteria for the extension were (1) to improve our space in and around the kitchen, (2) to add an extension that would improve the salability of the house, and (3) to keep within a given budget so we would not invest more than we could sell the house for, including a profit. The renovation-addition had to include (1) redoing the kitchen, (2) adding on an everyday eating area, (3) adding on a deck, and (4) adding on a garage or carport.—*Christopher and Priscilla Rodrigues*

ARCHITECTS' STATEMENT

Our new work encompassed five basic areas.
- The wing we added occupies prime space on the east elevation, taking advantage of the spectacular view.
- In order not to isolate the kitchen, we employed volume within and transparency through the new wing.
- The radial deck connects the living room and the new wing.
- The narrower porch provides direct kitchen access from the parking area below.
- The carport space below the elevated addition was a "dividend" created by the steep topography.
The lines, shapes, and materials of the existing house were reiterated in order to strengthen and eleborate on the sense of dormers cascading outward and downhill.
—*Shope Reno Wharton Associates*

veiled in a traditional skin. A contemporary addition in Colonial clothing, if you will.

All of these manipulations occurred behind the untouched placidity of the front facade. With a tight budget ($40,000) the architects opted for a ground-level carport (a garage without a full enclosure by walls but with a protecting roof) thus saving $6000. Since the spatial needs of the carport at ground level surpassed those of the new family room and dining area at first-floor level, decks were obviously the happy solution to unequal demands on the plan.

These decks connect the existing living room with the outside world for the first time while providing a new back door and mudroom entry, and the decks' low walls also serve to animate the "skin games" mentioned before.

Ceilings in the addition break the flat planes typical of standard housing and follow the angle of the new shed roof. With the elimination of a wall, the kitchen and new family room are spatially wed without being functionally compromised.

By selectively continuing one eave over the new back door and orienting the addition to an existing concave corner of the house exterior, the architects heightened the sense of transitional ambiguity between modern massing and traditional detailing. This project shows that if a mundane context is addressed as valid input in the design process, creative expression can be enhanced, not curtailed.

fig. 1 *Backyard view. Identical clapboard detailing aligned with the existing conditions helps order an expressive breaking of the Colonial box.*

fig. 2 *Front view, untouched. This sentinel of sobriety masks the events happening behind it.*

fig. 3 *Plan. By careful alignment, a new exterior stair, two decks, an eating-living area, and a mudroom and back door can exist in a minimal amount of square footage added on.*

fig. 4 *Linear linking of clapboard shadow lines is evidenced in this photograph.*

Photos and line drawings by the architects

1

2

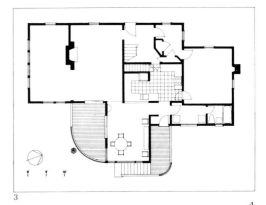
3   4

Focused Ego

*Arne Bystrom brings contemporary utility
and revived dignity to his own home.*

PROJECT PROFILE

Bystrom residence
Location: Seattle, Wash.
Architect: Arne Bystrom
Budget: $20,000
Area renovated: 800 ft²
Area added 100 ft²
(not including the 140-ft² deck)

OWNER-ARCHITECT'S
STATEMENT

Problem: To restore an historic Victorian residence, once the home of a territorial governor, which had suffered years of neglect, and at the same time to extend its use by making the house more harmonious with the lovely city lot on which it is located. To make the house more livable required making the kitchen larger and more usable in today's terms and providing more space for the family that would live in it while at the same time respecting the unique architectural style that the house represented.—*Arne Bystrom*

Architects are taught to question their world: evaluate, revise, and remake their environment. Society expects (and sometimes fears) that an architect will take a broad vision and bring skill, energy, and purpose to bear to create buildings that will boggle our understanding and vaporize the limits of our aesthetic experience. Potential clients expect that their needs will serve to bridle the architect's imperial ego.

So what happens when architects design for themselves? Unrestrained, violent effusions of creative insight? Monolithic statements of truth? Perhaps, but Arne Bystrom, a Seattle architect, chose to embrace a decoratively parched remnant of Victorian architecture with a sympathy seldom found in "modern" architects.

When Valerie and Arne Bystrom purchased their home, 90 percent of the original gingerbread ornamentation, turned columns, and interior detailing had been replaced with hardware-store stock items. Facing such a denuded shell, most of Arne Bystrom's contemporaries would have licked their chops and remade the house in their own image.

Fortunately for the building's spirit, Bystrom decided that he could revive the structure and adapt it without violating the spirit or letter of the aesthetic laws that had originally brought the house into being. The cost implications of this decision were enormously beneficial, as the entire budget was in the $20,000 range. Several basic decisions keyed future work. As Arne Bystrom puts it:

Early studies rejected out of hand a slavish museum reconstruction of the original house while the historic nature of the property ruled out as inappropriate the possibility of the remodeling being accomplished in an overlay style (such as High Tech/Victorian).

Therefore it was decided to do two things:

1. When the use was not changed (such as the front porch), to restore the structure as nearly as possible to the original within certain limitations such as no flocked wall paper in the entrance hall or gas lights hanging from the ceilings.

2. When the use was changed, such as the deck, the kitchen and the attic study, to design for today's needs and attitudes but from a palette of Victorian details.

Basically, several needs were addressed head on. The kitchen was woefully inadequate, the laundry room was combined with the bathroom, and there was a paucity of informal space. Typical twentieth-century revisions on the nineteenth-century program were effected to solve these problems with no major structural changes, thus saving money and following the guidelines Bystrom laid out for himself.

By adding a bay to the south, Arne Bystrom repeated the plan motif present in the living room to the north and allowed the kitchen to accept an informal dining area. By adding a wall in the bath-laundry room and reusing an existing closed-off doorway, he created two cozy rooms, each of single-use efficiency, at a small cost. By enclosing an existing porch, Bystrom reused original roof lines and created a back door and a mudroom cum plant sanctuary that further increased the area of the kitchen. In building a new deck to the east, Bystrom again chose to complement the existing house and to avoid strident self-expression. The deck's paucity of visual activity only reinforces the anachronism of the house's form and detailing. The new space created by the deck allows the house to grow in a functional sense without adding mass to the existing structure.

Fixed skylights were custom-built into the new bay and enclosed porch, avoiding the collision of the High Tech catalog and the custom carpentry of old. A more lyric representation of new needs being answered

1

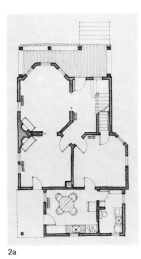

2a

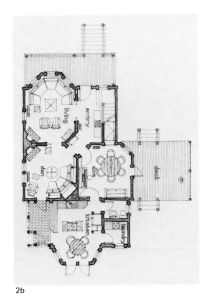

2b

3

fig. 1 *The realized scheme. The simple shed bay orients to the existing conditions effortlessly, while the eave moldings, porch glazing, and gable window all quietly embellish and enrich the existing form.*

fig. 2 *Floor plans, (a) existing and (b) revised. With the bay addition and porch enclosure to the south, the kitchen and informal dining area are brought into the twentieth century.*

fig. 3 *The existing southern end of the house. Note the lack of ornament and the ad hoc porch addition.*

Photos and line drawings by the architect

4a 4b 5

6

7

8

fig. 4 *(a) South elevation and (b) west elevation. Note the sympathetic detailing of the porch enclosure and the newly added gable windows.*

fig. 5 *Eave detailing. Historical research derived the gable gingerbread, and the quietly simplified eave-board fascia decoration articulates the roof lines with well-crafted elegance.*

fig. 6 *Kitchen interior, facing west. Open shelves, simple cabinet lines, and custom skylighting create a feeling of informal integration. Inexpensive alteration need not be ad hoc.*

fig. 7 *Kitchen interior, facing south. Skylighting is unobtrusive, and the millwork of the new bay is thoroughly integrated into that of the existing house. The line of the dropped beam supporting the wall removed at the juncture of the new bay is conveniently obscured by the pot hanger.*

fig. 8 *Gable windows, from the interior. The semifinished quality of this attic study is enhanced by the windows added by Arne Bystrom. Besides providing light, they are made operable to facilitate much-needed ventilation.*

can be seen in the five gable windows Bystrom inserted to allow light into the semicivilized attic. These utilitarian portals could have been mere triangles articulating some abstract structural form, but by using delightful, well-crafted details, Bystrom turned them into expressively ornamental features.

Throughout the interior, oak millwork was either restored or created; the new kitchen cabinets wrap around the overtly new appliances, serving to mitigate the collision between a nineteenth-century house and twentieth-century technology.

Arne Bystrom added glazing to the south to increase the house's passive solar gain. But beyond this gesture, an in-teresting insight into the energy utility of the house is considered by Bystrom.

Victorian houses were, in their way, designed to be energy efficient in that all of the rooms were able to be closed off and heated only when used. Also, these rooms were scaled for the use of family groups (11 to 14 feet on a side) so that no more area per room was heated than necessary. In addition, the walls, roof, and floor were insulated to local (Seattle) standards.

It is the architect's willingness to see beyond the power of personal expression into the legitimate beauty and utility of the past that makes this addition so welcome. How many architects have the courage to let tradition and history have an impact on their work? Far too few.

Less Is More

*Chad Floyd reduces the volume of a house
and increases the usable space.*

PROJECT PROFILE

Gahagan residence
Location: New England
Architect: Chad Floyd,
Moore Grover Harper;
Steve Lloyd, project manager
Budget: $125,000
Area renovated: 1600 ft^2
(including demolition)
Area added: 300 ft^2

Imagine having a single home be the architectural focus for your family since 1746. For eight continuous generations, the Gahagan family had lived in and loved their New England farmhouse.

As times changed, the house was added onto, creating an "ell" extending to the east. The additions were sometimes insubstantial, sometimes subtantial, but always deferential to the parent building. It was with this legacy that the latest family members to occupy the house decided that their way of living was incompatible with some parts of their treasured home.

Almost predictably, the chief source of misfit occurred in the kitchen. It's a bit ironic that Fritz and Alva Gahagan wanted to have what was typically present in an eighteenth-century farmhouse but often removed in the Victorian era—a large, open eat-in kitchen. Additionally, a new laundry room, half bath, and potting shed were needed.

But more than wanting to simply accommodate new appliances and an informal lifestyle, the Gahagans wanted to build an energy-efficient addition that would generate as much heat from burning wood and passive solar gain as possible.

Despite the obvious need for change, the Gahagans wanted to maintain a continuity and respect for the existing ancestral home. It is with these somewhat conflicting desires that they approached Chad Floyd, an architect with the firm of Moore Grover Harper.

It was clear to Floyd that the problem was not one of inadequate space but one of too much space being thoughtlessly added over the years. The existing structure was unsuitable for the new occupants, and some of it had to be removed. By carefully removing some structure, preserving other

OWNERS' STATEMENT

The renovation was conceived around several firm assumptions. The original house and the lines of all existing additions would not be altered. The interior, centered around the kitchen, would be functional, open and bright, and heated by wood and sun but could not clash with the original house. Likewise the exterior, while containing a large amount of glass, could not clash with or dominate the original house.

To accomplish this without stifling the project, we purposefully chose an architect whose concepts were much broader than our own conservative stance and set aside nine months to resolve the contradictions inherent in our approaches.

We believe we obtained what we wanted—an addition that exists peacefully with the original structure yet has its own excitement and atmosphere.—*The Gahagans*

ARCHITECT'S STATEMENT

What became urgent in the design of the Gahagan addition was the search for an architecture that might stand nicely alongside the existing, very distinguished, traditional structure while still sporting enough perkiness to give the impression that we architects had been around.

After a couple of false starts that found us, predictably, flexing our muscles too much, we settled on an approach that took delight in rather than exception to the considerable qualities of the old house.

—*Chad Floyd*

parts, and adding wholly new elements, Floyd was able to engender a delightful ambiguity of old and new.

Essentially, the southern half of the existing "ell" was demolished, leaving the northerly garage, the existing foundation, and a small chimney. With the footprint of the work already determined by the remaining foundation, Floyd began to reinterpret the pieces and parts that make up the elements of eighteenth-century Colonial building.

The exterior form of the addition was aligned with the existing south wall and presented a very straightforward massing. The siding, roofing, paint, and windows duplicated existing conditions in form and detailing.

On the interior, 8 × 8 inch posts and beams were used as the main structural components in the new south-facing, double-height space, but they are slightly oversized for the loading involved and clustered in such a way as to proudly display their simple Constructivist aesthetic. Similarly, the southern glazing takes the small pane windows of traditional Colonial architecture through several transformations and permutations. Lastly and most impressively, the central chimney asserts the traditional form normally hidden behind walls and plaster.

The finishes used heighten the effect of playful assertiveness. With all surfaces painted white, save the fireplace, floor, and furnishings, a quieting unity is imposed, dampening the potential for visual chaos given the power of the bared post-and-beam construction, and the fireplace is highlighted. Made of recovered granite cobblestones, its raw, natural expressiveness proclaims its traditional posture as the heart of the Colonial home. Chad Floyd based

1

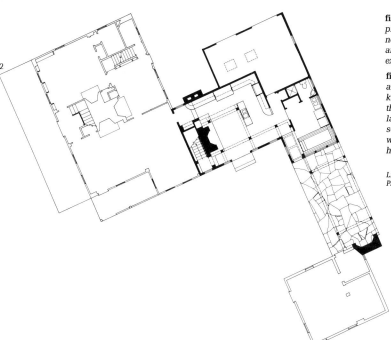

2

fig. 1 *Exterior. Flanked by existing structures, the addition presents a simple form, identical surface treatments, and a new focus of double doors (center), clearly expressing itself and yet thoroughly subdominant to the formal front of the existing house.*

fig. 2 *First-floor plan. The black lines indicate areas affected by the project. At the center of the plan, the new kitchen faces south and serves as a transition space between the formal first floor of the existing house and the new laundry, potting-shed, bath, and patio spaces to the east and south. Note the remnant chimney and new patio to the south, which serve as reminders of the removed portions of the house.*

Line drawings by the architect
Photos by Cervin Robinson

fig. 3 *South wall. A symmetrical facade centers on the new double doors. Note the bowed opening, which is the only curve present in the entire house exterior. Note also the strip array of traditional small pane windows, stock items made powerful by their organization, subtly levitating the roof from the clapboard body of the house. The post-and-beam structure to the right pops through the gable-end wall with a minimum of fanfare.*

fig. 4 *Isometric. Flanked by the two existing chimneys, the new chimney and steps form the focus of the new addition. The new post-and-beam work extends outside over the new patio space.*

fig. 5 *Arbor. This west-facing patio has its view framed and its space defined by the literal extension of the post-and-beam structural system from the inside. Note the traditional lap joints and pegged construction. The patio's perimeter follows the outline of a removed addition, and the new arbor effectively evokes an image of bared bones in remembrance of an addition gone—but not forgotten.*

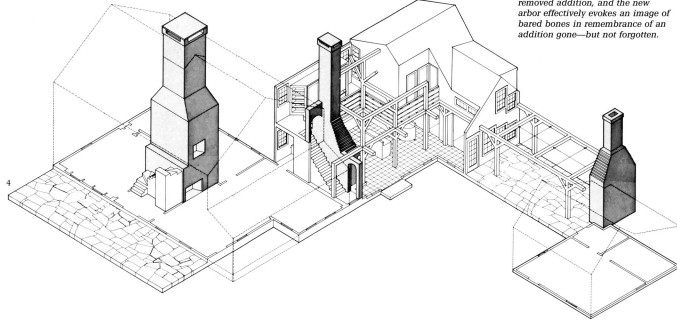

5

the form, location, and detailing of the chimney on careful research into the period of the original home.

It is with this basis of knowledge that Floyd was able to achieve his quietly symbolic intentions. The gentle assertion of the post-and-beam structure up into the two-story solar-heated convection space and out into the newly created exterior court elegantly clarifies the essence of Colonial construction. The bared chimney is allowed to expose its form and material—even when it passes through the roof, where skylights reveal the traditional transition from interior masonry to exterior brickwork.

But beyond these civilized caricatures, this project relies on the essential tool of spatial manipulation. With the post-and-beam construction isolated within a generous space, this normally hidden structure takes on a sculptural sensibility. It is within this small yet somehow grand space that Floyd's clever quirks are allowed to happen gracefully.

fig. 6 *Balcony. As structure and chimney reach the clerestory level, their animation takes on new life. The masonry mass twists to embrace the existing wall (right) for lateral support and to frame the head of the stairs. The oversized cross bracing seems to spring forth to the heavens, while downstairs the similar knee bracing was quite restrained. Note the subtly located spotlights. By allowing windows, beams, masonry, railings, etc., to bypass each other in a considered coincidence, the architect creates a rich choreography to fill the space and catch the light.*

fig. 7 *Sun space. To create both a spatial and structural event, the architect manipulated the scale of the post-and-beam structure, allowing the members to be a bit oversized, abnormally clustered, and thoroughly distinct from any wall. Note that the overcoat of white paint serves to mute the potential for hyperkinetic activity while helping to expose the dramatic checking (cracks due to shrinkage) of the wood members. Note also the clear visual shot through to the extreme end of the potting shed in the left center of the photo.*

6

7

fig. 8 *(Opposite) Fireplace. Framed by the lattice of semisculptured timber structure, the sheer mass of this granite chimney is quite grand. The traditional stepped angle to the left would be invisible in a traditional application but is allowed to catch the light cascading down from the skylights above. Similarly liberated, flanking extensions serve to frame openings—to the left, access to the existing house; to the right, an in-chimney barbeque. The black slate flooring serves to pick up some passive solar gain from the southern exposure. Despite the fact the fireplace is of the optimally efficient Rumsford design, the owners opted to maximize heating efficiency with a wood stove.*

Congenial Complexity

Harry Teague creates a High Tech–Victorian
extension to an Aspen, Colorado, home.

PROJECT PROFILE

Salter residence
Location: Aspen, Colo.
Architect: Harry Teague
Budget: $40,000
Area renovated: 40 ft²
Area added: 800 ft²

Jim Salter needed to add a bedroom to the mining-town Victorian house he had restored. He contacted local architect Harry Teague, and the plans rapidly took shape.

Teague had designed a lushly variated first-floor master bedroom, complete with a fireplace, reading nook, two exterior exits, and a skylight. Above that was a small garret defined by steeply pitched roofs. The design was so appealing to Jim Salter that he decided he wanted to share the benefits of it with a larger group of people; he abandoned the idea of a bedroom retreat and switched design programs in midstream. Salter opted to create an informal kitchen-dining-living space without any major changes in the basic design. Cabinets and appliances replaced the bed, the dressing area became an informal dining room, and the reading nook became, well, a reading nook.

Having more than the ability to be functionally versatile, Teague's design uses slightly exaggerated Victorian motifs to create an energy-independent addition that is at home with its neighbors.

The form of the house has three parts, which are in turn developed. The first floor contains two small porches, the result of beveled wall planes pulling back from the perimeter. Above this angling first story a low-pitched porch-style roof mirrors its counterpart on the existing house. And atop the low-pitched roof, again following the formal motif of the existing house, is a steeply pitched roof enclosing the aforementioned garret.

The shallow porches of the first floor are actually designed to be used as deep overhangs creating shade to prevent overheating during the summer months. The steeply pitched garret roof has its angle (different

OWNER'S STATEMENT

This small Victorian house stands on a corner lot in the residential section of Aspen. Built in the 1880s, it had completely deteriorated when it was restored in 1972. The restoration was not old-maidish. The original lines of the house, moldings, windows, doors, and other details were retained, but within there was removal of walls and even ceilings to create light and space. Still, when finished, the house was small—just one real bedroom and bath. There was a tiny basement and limited storage space.

The addition which Harry Teague designed was intended to almost double the size and to join to the old house a modern structure that would also serve as a kind of new basis and buttress. Although it was to be harmonious with the older portion, it did not attempt to reproduce it. The result was a jolt of technology and line that revitalized everything. Solar heat via radiant hot water, a Japanese bath, and a beautiful second floor bedroom with a cruciform ceiling and views in four directions including the ski mountain are some of the successful features.

Admirable from both without and within, it has transformed a small jewel into a kind of oceanliner which should be afloat for at least another century.—*James Salter*

ARCHITECT'S STATEMENT

The addition to Jim Salter's renovated mining-town Victorian house was meant to live comfortably with its Victorian neighbors in a quiet Aspen neighborhood and to take advantage of Colorado's plentiful sunshine for energy savings. Set back from the original structure, somewhat behind a tree and a small cabin, the addition borrows lines, roof pitches, and windows from the original house.

The solar energy requirements were resolved by careful window arrangement within the Victorian framework and the use of recessed solar panels in the perfectly oriented roofs.

The completed addition exudes the quality of warmth that seems to happen with an owner's intimate involvement.—*Harry Teague*

from the existing house) determined by the optimum solar-gain orientation for the active solar heating system it supports. Also mounted on the steeply pitched roof is an inset dormer. As if emerging from within, this delightful little element serves to contain, at its base, a skylight, illuminating the dressing area cum dining table.

All of this variation is related to the existing building by the use of similar windows, siding, and geometries.

The interior is as expressively articulated as the exterior. The first floor contains a simple galley-style kitchen; the dining area facing a brick screen disguised as a fireplace houses the addition's main source of heat, a wood stove, and the reading nook. As mentioned, the walls angle back and forth to define the porches and create the overhang, but the breaks act in concert with the pseudo fireplace mass to divide the interior in an effective and yet informal way.

Above this multipurpose first floor sit a multitude of angled planes defining a delightfully eccentric garret sleeping space. The visual activity of the converging planes is heightened by the ubiquitous overlay of beaded tongue-and-groove siding on every surface save the floor.

Good design can embrace many criteria and many changes. This addition was lucky in that its first alteration occurred before it had a chance to get built. Similarly, the overlay of solar utility and energy-efficient design is happily embraced by the mining-town Victorian geometries. It was not simply luck that enabled Jim Salter to accommodate so much in so little. It was his decision to hire a good architect and work diligently with him to derive his affably convoluted addition.

1

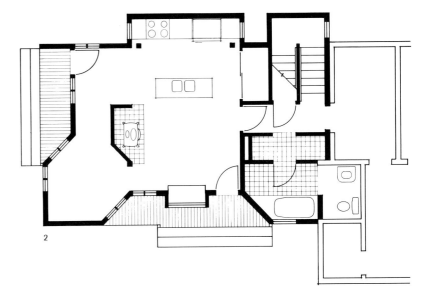

2

fig. 1 *East elevation. Capturing morning light, this form echoes the existing gable end to the right. The arched opening, shaped shingles, and ornamental brickwork on the chimney present the multiple foci of a Victorian aesthetic.*

fig. 2 *First-floor plan. The convoluted walls angle back to create shallow porches that protect from solar overheating in summer. Note that the top recess used so well for the counter was to accept a bed originally, while the reading nook at lower left remained unchanged.*

Photos and line drawing by the architect

3

fig. 3 *Kitchen-dining area. The focus and divider of the space, the chimney is a sham, merely an envelope of brick enclosing the wood stove and its flue. Note the exposed joist diffusing the light from the skylight above. Note also that the post-and-beam major structural members are allowed to express themselves.*

fig. 4 *South elevation. Loosely attached to the existing house in an effort to maintain distance from an existing shed and tree, the addition, with its similar materials, geometries, and scale, thoroughly integrates the new (center) with the old (right). Note the inset dormer and solar panels set to the perfect winter heating angle.*

fig. 5 *Stair. The new stair connecting kitchen and garret is made interesting by the main framing member serving as a skeletal reminder that the stair is indeed an applied shed extension to the basic form of the addition.*

fig. 6 *Garret. Beaded tongue-and-groove siding covers a multitude of angles reflecting the underside of the convoluted roof form.*

4

5

A California Corner

Leon Armantrout customizes a prefabricated house.

PROJECT PROFILE

Armantrout residence
Location: Redlands, Calif.
Architect: Leon Armantrout,
Day & Armantrout
Budget: $80,000
Area renovated: 986 ft^2
Area added: 800 ft^2

When Margie and Leon Armantrout discovered a small house in Redlands, California, the building was less impressive than the location and the mature trees surrounding it. An area of 986 square feet could not begin to adequately house a growing family. The building was a 1924 kit home, made from parts marketed by the Pacific Redicut Home Company. Fortunately, Leon Armantrout just happened to be an architect, and he saw a simple solution.

Besides the straightforward need to resurface and repair the existing structure, Armantrout realized that his kit home just did not have the capacity to accommodate a 1980s kitchen and the informal dining and living space that go along with it. The area for an addition was staked out by the presence of a patio. To accommodate the new construction, an existing lean-to addition had to be removed.

The simple single-story house did not need a grand gesture that might prove demeaning to the original building and its neighbors. Instead, Leon Armantrout saw the potential in a simple extension of the existing roof. Fortunately, the existing eave height off the ground was several feet higher than normal for a single-story house because the floor was also raised above the ground plane. So the simple extension of the existing roof plane provided a substantial spatial increase without a change in roof pitch. By extending this plane beyond the side walls of the existing home, Armantrout was able to wrap his addition around the original building and make a living area with three exposed sides. With the roof extension providing the exterior form of the

OWNER-ARCHITECT'S STATEMENT

Concerned with restoring the house and adapting it to the needs of our growing family, we designed an 800-square-foot wood and glass addition consisting of a living-dining-cooking pavilion 4 feet below the existing structure. The change in elevation was indicated by the slope of the site. The original bedrooms and bath were retained, and the original kitchen-dining space converted to a sleeping loft, which overlooks the new living area with its freestanding fireplace. The original living room became a family-music room with its former front doors now opening onto the east yard, which contains a number of fruit trees.—*Leon Armantrout*

addition, Armantrout decided to make the interior an event. Beneath the simple roof plane, large-sized glazing brings the outside in. In the same vein, Armantrout had sliding glass walls made to open up the addition to the existing patio.

In creating such an open interior volume of space, Armantrout created a collision with the existing corner of the building. To soften the impact, he removed the corner walls and replaced them with two custom columns. The low walls that remain offer a visual barrier from the living room within the existing home, while allowing the space to flow from old to new without an awkward break. Armantrout reused the existing bedroom space turned balcony as a sleeping loft for children or guests.

By bringing the existing clapboard inside the addition and negating the existing corner of the building, Armantrout helped create a meshing of modern space with existing materials. The architect aligned the addition's concrete floor with the existing patio and used the window walls mentioned to further extend the quiet sense of ambiguity to include the limits of the newly enclosed space.

By simplifying the scale and detailing of the kitchen, organizing the lighting and heating systems in a simple ceiling element, and refusing to clutter his space with unnecessary furnishings, Armantrout lets the space itself do the talking.

In recognizing the spatial power of the open plan, Leon Armantrout opted to reject a pat answer to a classic addition form and created an overtly modern solution without destroying the scale or character of a Pacific Redicut original.

1

2

fig. 1 *Interior, facing the kitchen. The custom Y columns allow the newly created space to flow over the remaining low wall at the original house's once-exterior corner. Glazing is in the form of infill glass panels creating the lightest of touches on the existing building's mass. With the continuation of the exterior siding inside, a clear mesh of new and old is created. Lighting and air circulation occur in the plenum dropped from the new roof peak, integrating with the connection of the new Y columns. By simplifying such elements, Armantrout makes the space itself rather than the detailing of the envelope the dominant design feature.*

fig. 2 *Living room end. A modern sense of minimal structure and maximum openness is achieved in the new portion of the house. The large beams integrated with the heating and electrical plenum at the top of the picture have the capacity to carry the roof load back to the Y column seen in the upper left without the imposition of columns or walls into the open plan. Note the tensile cross bracing in the window bay behind the fireplace.*

Line drawing by the architect
Photos by Darrow M. Watt

3

4

5

fig. 3 *Existing conditions. Note the bay that was removed and the existing patio that served as the floor level for the new addition.*

fig. 4 *A simple extension of the roof plane creates an almost imperceptible addition. Sliding glass walls serve to transform the living room into an extension of the patio. Note that the eave detailing of exposed rafter ends duplicates the existing conditions.*

fig. 5 *Kitchen connection. As was done in the sleeping loft, the entire wall here was eliminated to create a direct spacial connection with the existing house. The new entry aligns with the new stair access to the existing home, making an implicit circulation path that helps define the kitchen area. Note that the refrigerator nestles into a new void in the existing wall. Note also the integration of the new wall at left with the Y column. The skylight breaks a potentially oppressive ceiling plane. The little strip of incandescent light bulbs follows the underside of the new beaming and indicates the new axis that is about to be encountered.*

fig. 6 *Plan diagram. The dotted area indicates the addition. Note the new stair to the family room and the dotted line indicating the removed corner walls.*

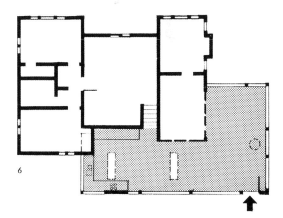

6

The Lightest Touch

Richard Fernau and Laura Hartman seem to do almost nothing and yet completely reorient a farmhouse in rural Maryland.

PROJECT PROFILE

Swaner-Nichols residence
Location: Howard County, Md.
Architects: Fernau-Hartman
Budget: $70,000
Area renovated: 1000 ft^2
Area added: 160 ft^2

Architects by their nature and training are advocates. A generation ago, they advocated the rejection of the past in favor of their view of the future. It was simple for those architects to say "No!" like the newly emboldened two-year-old celebrating the recent conquest of language. The architects of our era have had the failures of that unbridled egotism rubbed in their faces.

If anything, the strident advocacy of old has been replaced by a sensitivity among contemporary architects toward the individual sets of values and rules generated by each new problem they face. Perhaps an aesthetic relativism and a growing respect for flexibility may just help architects to become the resourceful innovators they studied in school rather than witless ciphers reciting dogma.

It is with these sensibilities that Richard Fernau and Laura Hartman, two young architects from California, journeyed to a rural Maryland farmhouse to investigate the owners' request for help. Karan Swaner and Wylie Nichols knew their farmhouse needed work but assumed that to renovate their modest house they had to perform an aggressive remodeling involving some added square footage.

The house was too dark, too cluttered, and too small, faced the wrong way, and was energy-inefficient. Most architects, young or old, would listen to this litany and assume the form of the house must be reworked to address these problems.

Two things stood in the path of radical revision. First, the clients had a latent desire to maintain a harmonious relationship with the nearby manor house this little farmhouse once served. Second, in a classic role reversal, the architects were revolted by the idea that they would be the ones to ruin the timeless informality of the existing building.

OWNERS' STATEMENT

Our aim in remodeling was to give our farmhouse a more workable floor plan without upstaging the nearby manor house on which it once depended. We also wanted to "turn the house around" so that it would look out toward the property and the southern sunshine rather than toward the street. The biggest problem was the kitchen, which was dark, bleak, and small, cut by the steep, turning staircase.

We began by considering venturesome additions, which not only were financially unfeasible but risked clashing with the modest scale of the house as well. The architects convinced us that our budget would be better spent within the house's original framework.

From the outside, it is still the original farmhouse; inside it is now spacious, sunny, and far more habitable.
—*Karan Swaner and Wylie Nichols*

ARCHITECT'S STATEMENT

We strove in the Swaner-Nichols remodel toward invisibility rather than toward making a conspicuous mark on the house. Perhaps because of its distance from California—historically and climatically as well as geographically—we had an exaggerated respect for its type and were reluctant to tamper with it. Strictly speaking, the house was far from typologically pure; no fewer than three remodelings had been visited upon it in the past; however, the original logic of the one-room section and the T-shaped plan was still apparent. In the end, it was the simplicity of that logic, combined with the timeless desirability of light, warmth, and a cooling breeze that gave us our direction.

Without being a slavish restoration, it is pleasing to us that our efforts on the Swaner-Nichols farmhouse can be enjoyed without being seen.—*Richard Fernau*

Architects have traditionally regarded existing buildings with a cavalier disregard for their present condition. Familiarity with construction techniques breeds a contempt for the mistakes of the past and usually fosters the bold strokes required to bring utility and delight to an ill-conceived or clumsily altered building.

But in this particular case, the architects, bold in their native California, felt enough reverence for this demure farmhouse to apply their skills in a way that actually obscured their impact on the building.

In no way was this a studied preservationist reconstruction. The very nature of a complete reorganization away from the street, recognizing both the passive solar gain and the view to the south, was a radical departure from any preservationist's criteria for authentic rehabilitation.

Rather than search their hearts and minds for a new truth or study the historical material available for the old truth, Fernau and Hartman became intimate with the existing structure in order to find the timeless truth of its compelling innocence. Keyed by this consciousness, several modest changes affected the entire house.

An imposing stair was removed from the kitchen, and a new stair was built in the center of the house. With the stair out of the kitchen, more light was allowed into the house and the kitchen itself could expand without needing an addition. The new stair was positioned to serve as a light well and a spatial hub for the house—qualities that have tangible spiritual implications. Located adjacent to two new windows, it also serves as a flue to vent overheated or stale air.

The need for informal dining space was met by reclaiming an existing sun-porch addition from near collapse. By refitting the existing shell with new windows and open-

fig. 1 *The house. Seemingly untouched by modern hands, this remarkable farmhouse radiates a timeless sense of comfort and common sense. The sun porch was completely renovated, the vertical mass at its end simplified. Of the five second-story windows above the porch, only one is original.*

Line drawings by the architects
Photos by Stuart Pregnall

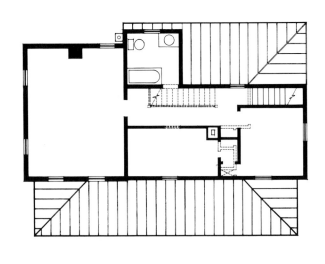
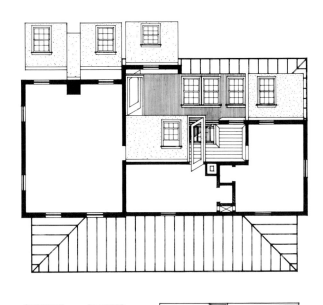

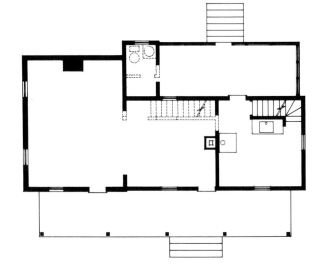
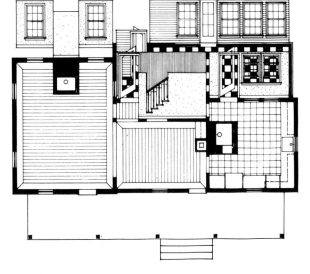

2

3

ing up new interior windows into the kitchen and living room, the architects turned the renovated porch into the lens focusing the orientation of the occupants toward the pastoral backyard view. Simultaneously, south light filters through the space, into the surrounding rooms, diffusing its glare in the summer and distributing its heat in the winter. An ambiguity between new and old was created by using windows, trim, and materials identical to those present in the existing house for all new openings. In salvaging this unheated and neglected space, the architects eliminated the need for a completely new addition.

The only exterior alterations implemented were some additional windows placed toward the southerly view and minor resurfacing to remove inconsistencies caused by three prior remodelings. All the moves made were executed with a logic and technique indistinguishable from the original farmhouse design.

In their effort to renovate without obvious remodeling, Fernau and Hartman retain the traditional role of advocate architects. Their advocacy was turned away from their egos and took up the cause of rekindling the existing farmhouse's latent spirit and power. By covering their tracks so well, Fernau and Hartman evidence a sophistication and expertise that redefines the role of contemporary architects acting in concert with an existing building.

They have achieved a bloodless coup, a silent revolution, and the echoes of their light touch on this house will be heard for generations to come for those who care to listen.

4

fig. 2   Plans and elevations (existing to the left, revised to the right). The south elevation is shown on the top. Note increased glazing and shades. The second floor is shown in the middle; the first floor, on the bottom. First-floor new construction is indicated as dashed lines. Note new elements shown as flipped-up parts to the right.

fig. 3   The stair. Completely new, this formal, functional, and spiritual centerpiece distributes southerly light and vents air via the new second-story window array. Note that the interior window to the left is new, as is all the wall work around the stair.

fig. 4   The sun porch. All windows shown are new. The two interior windows were made possible by the movement of the stair. Only the tile and furnishings bespeak of a recent remodeling.

Swaner-Nichols Residence   35

Backyard Event

*A boisterous new back door and greenhouse
enliven a Chevy Chase, Maryland, home.*

PROJECT PROFILE

Wilson residence
Location: Bethesda, Md.
Architect: Mark McInturff,
Wiebenson & McInturff, Architects
Budget: $60,000
Area renovated: 400 ft^2
Area added: 170 ft^2

Gerald and Marjorie Wilson wanted a new kitchen. They realized that to get the kitchen they wanted, some space had to be added to their Georgian-style house in the suburbs of Washington, D.C., and for that reason they called in architect Mark McInturff as a consultant to confirm that their desires were feasible. They had no intention of hiring anyone to design their remodeling, but with several bold conceptual strokes, McInturff rendered himself indispensable.

Normally people consider an architect to be either an irrational artist who prevents a project's utility or a master technician who solves complex problems with a vast body of knowledge. The Wilsons thought their desires were so pragmatic and their problems so straightforward that an additional layer of thought was not needed. But they quickly realized that their proposed project need not be limited to the straightforward renovation of their kitchen.

Architects cannot help but apprehend the larger scale of a building's organization when they confront an existing house. The flaws obvious to them are accepted by the occupants who over the years have grown blind to the inconveniences or inadequacies. Walls can be quite powerful unless one has the training and vision to see beyond their undeniable presence.

The Wilsons had never questioned the circulation pattern of their house—and why should they? It was, after all, a substantial suburban dwelling of classic lines and solid construction. But when Mark McInturff entered the house, he realized that the center of the first-floor plan, crowded with closets and the entry stair, created an indirect flow of traffic causing people to walk through the formal dining room and kitchen to get to or from the backyard or bathroom. This first reaction to the house was the furthest

OWNERS' STATEMENT

We began thinking about an addition to gain more eating space and a modernized kitchen and to change the flow of traffic through the kitchen. We felt that the job was so straightforward as not to justify the expense of an architect. Nevertheless, we asked Mark McInturff for a few preliminary suggestions. He came up with a plan that changed our simple concept to a truly revolutionary modification of our home. We discovered that the new approach would increase the total cost only modestly.

Our house is so improved that it feels and functions as a new house, with everything exactly the way we wanted it. All the long hours of planning and living through the inconvenience of the actual work were well worth the effort. We are completely happy with our decision to modify our home rather than move to a larger house.—*Gerald and Marjorie Wilson*

ARCHITECT'S STATEMENT

This project involves both an addition to the house and a clarification of the existing plan. We were asked, as we so frequently are, to revise the present kitchen and add a breakfast and sitting space and to provide new access to a recently built terrace in the backyard.

Our solution involved recognizing and extending the existing center hall through the house. By simply moving some old closets and storage, we allowed the former front hall to continue through the house as in more gracious Georgian precedents. In the new plan, movement through the house no longer compromises the rooms.—*Mark McInturff*

thought from the Wilsons' mind, but ultimately it was the insight that ordered the entire scheme.

By simply removing all obstructions between the front door and the backyard, a spine of circulation space was created. The existing bath remained unchanged, the new kitchen stayed in the same location as the original, but the closets were removed and relocated in the new addition. Having resolved the functional problems of the existing plan, McInturff could focus his energies on the addition needed to accommodate the new back door, closet, and eating area.

The architect realized that the new circulation axis he created needed an exciting terminus as much as the backyard needed a focal point. In response McInturff created a dynamic portico facing the garden. Access was via glazed double doors, which also provided the visual lure needed to reward the visitor upon entry from the street.

With the portico locked into its location as the grand finale to the entry axis, McInturff next addressed the original problem that motivated the Wilsons to consider an addition in the first place, the kitchen and dining area. The original galley layout of the kitchen worked well, but unfortunately the appliances were outdated and existing counter space was required.

Generally the trend in upscaling major appliances equates to an increase in quantity, and this kitchen is no exception. Bigger appliances mean less counter space unless new space is found. Since one side of the galley kitchen abutted the half bath and the other side was limited by the garage wall, McInturff had to make a choice.

Moving a bathroom involves several trades, but moving a wall involves far less time and effort—hence, less money. The potential problem arises when the reduced space created on the back of the moved wall

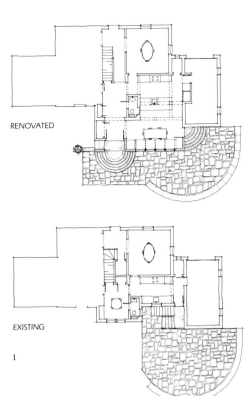

RENOVATED

EXISTING

1

fig. 1 *Floor plans. The existing formal entry at the top of the plan is crowded by a closet and twisted stair window. By straightening the stair and removing two closets, the architect created an entry axis. Note that the bath and kitchen maintain their locations and layout even though both were renovated. Note that the existing patio was extended to meet the new back door and that the cascading steps down from the new addition to ground level follow the semicircular pattern of the existing low wall.*

fig. 2 *Exterior. The two forms of portico and greenhouse meet with a crisp directness. Note the caricatured broken pediment and column profile "of an inflated classical pretense—celebrating the connection to the garden" (the words of the architect). Note the continuity of the brick (serving as the plinth for the addition) with the existing house.*

Photos and line drawings by the architect

fig. 3 *Sketch. The manipulated form of the portico can be seen in this sketch. Note how the formal event works both as a terminus to an interior axis and as a beckoning focal point for the backyard.*

fig. 4 *Sink centerline. Fake broken beaming (articulated by the use of color), glazing patterns, and light-fixture orientation all respect the sink centerline—even the goldfish get into the act. Note the insulating shades on the new glazing.*

fig. 5 *Kitchen. Walls are removed, leaving a column and dropped beams for support above. Note the recessed refrigerator and oven to the extreme left.*

3

4

5

in question is inadequate. In this case, the back space was a garage, and McInturff was able to impose the 2½ feet needed to recess the new refrigerator and ovens while leaving just enough space for a midsize car. Without the impact of the energy crisis, this kitchen may have taken a different form.

Since the existing kitchen organization worked well for the owner, McInturff saw no reason to relocate the position of the sink or the range, and it was the sink location that in turn oriented the form of the informal dining area of the addition space. The tasks done at a sink are not joyous. Those locked in place by these tasks appreciate a view to ponder.

Since the space opposite the sink needed to have greenhouse glazing to bring in enough natural light for the newly recessed kitchen, McInturff centered his five individual bays of windows and skylights on the sink, providing the centered sense of a building responding to the needs of the user. This alignment was enhanced by some ornamental beam extensions broken over the centerline of the sink.

The exterior form of the addition reflects the dual identity of vertically oriented portico and inherently horizontal greenhouse. The forms simply abut each other in a mutually enhancing composition. Since their scale and functions were unprecedented in the existing house form, McInturff felt free to create a construction that had few roots in the original building. The single linking feature is the exposed whitewashed brick serving as the foundation for the new addition.

When contemplating an addition, home owners run the risk of thinking of their house as a fait accompli, an immutable given. Hence additions are often bloated distensions of spaces added without an eye toward renovating the original structure in a way that reduces the net volume of space added.

To create a solution that both revives and enriches the existing structure as well as adds to it takes an educated objectivity simply unavailable to the occupant of the building. The Wilsons had their eyes opened by the vision of Mark McInturff and discovered that their entire house could become the beneficiary of a 170-square-foot addition.

Rear Renovation

By adding all of 14 square feet, Mark McInturff makes sense of an entire house.

PROJECT PROFILE

Compton residence
Location: Washington, D.C.
Architect: Mark McInturff,
Wiebenson & McInturff, Architects
Budget: $35,000
Area renovated: 600 ft^2
Area added: 14 ft^2

When Sarah Compton bought her town house in Washington, D.C., she knew what she was in for. Having tackled several remodelings before, she understood the implications involved in removing the previous owner's several attempts to civilize an aging nineteenth-century town house. She also knew that the jumbled walls and extraordinarily dim spaces needed an order that defied an initial inspection. Besides such abstract practicalities as light, order, and space, she knew that she could not live without a "real" kitchen.

By definition, the typical row house cannot have natural lighting from any walls save the front and the back. Despite the lack of light, this particular row house had two internal rooms, creating five occupiable spaces in a 600-square-foot first floor.

Sarah Comptom brought in an architect, Mark McInturff, to organize the clutter. Mark saw the latent potential in the almost prototypical plan of the house. In terms of plan organization, the street side of the house had the normal minor bay of the entry and stair and the larger living room bay between its parallel bearing walls. The back of the house was a single-height wing, an extension of the living room bay. More than likely an earlier addition, the rear portion of the building had no spatial connection with the front two-thirds of the house. Separating the two parts were a half bath and a rear entry porch, leaving an arbitrarily located door as the only connection between front and back.

Much had to be removed before any order or spatial freedom could be realized. McInturff condensed the bath, laundry, and circulation path into the minor entry-stair

OWNER'S STATEMENT

My house had been horribly and cheaply "redone" by an earlier owner. It was a disaster. The kitchen was dark, inefficient, and cramped. The first-floor rooms were awkwardly divided; the dining room had no natural light. A nearly unusable bedroom was stuck on the end of a long, narrow corridor behind the dining room. A bizarrely shaped bathroom was sandwiched in between.

The house needed more light and more continuity. I wanted a large, bright kitchen (figuring someday I might learn to cook), and I wanted a powder room and the laundry (which was occupying a large and lovely space upstairs) on the first floor.

—*Sarah Compton*

ARCHITECT'S STATEMENT

The Compton house is actually a remodeling of a remodeling. Only a few years earlier, a previous owner had completed a sort of item-by-item remodeling that succeeded in ruining all the remaining detail without improving the dark and claustrophobic plan. Our client, who had remodeled several houses before this one, knew that more substantial work would be needed to provide the light, open house and large kitchen she wanted.

Our solution (as with many of our house projects) was to create—or recreate—a path through the house that does not compromise the rooms and to put new focus on, and give access to, a private garden in the rear.

—*Mark McInturff*

bay at the front of the house. He removed all interior walls save the single masonry wall separating front and rear. Having literally cleaned house, the architect applied an order to these two unrelated spaces by one simple addition of space.

Where once a back door entry alcove had prohibited through circulation along the stairway side of the building, McInturff enclosed that 14 square feet and instantly created a 60-foot axis through the entire house. Modest spaces were connected by a single grand vista, organized by the rear wing's north wall and an interior colonnade created by the architect to replace the original bearing wall that had divided the stair-entry bay from the living room bay. Circulation was no longer a space-consuming divider of rooms but a unifying orientation, a clarifying axis that was possessed by all interior spaces.

These general plan revisions helped create the eat-in kitchen Sarah Compton had always wanted. Due to McInturff's decongestive reorganization, the entire rear wing could be allocated as a spacious area for cooking, dining, and informal entertaining.

In order to fully expand and realize the potential for his newly ordered axis, the architect allowed for a proper culmination of its explicit path in a revitalized backyard. This could only be accomplished by removing most of the rear wall and by installing a doorway-window that releases the energy of the axis. When combined with a lightly explosive exterior facade facing the new backyard, the results are thoroughly expressive of an energetic imagination and a positive vision of what a building can be.

fig. 1 *Backyard elevation. An uplifting gesture that invites entry was created by removing 80 percent of the brick wall facing the garden and breaking the cornice. The remaining walls are almost archeological in nature, a remnant frame for a new construction. The lightly formal steps make a transition in scale into the heightened facade. The newly inserted wall is as animated as the remaining fragments are dull, culminating in a void centered over the new doorway. (The raised cornice is to serve as part of a rail for a future roof deck).*

fig. 2 *Axonometrics, (a) before and (b) after. The architect encountered a disorganized glut of walls. Circulation led to no apparent end, and the backyard was a patch of dirt seen from one small window. By removing all nonbearing walls and replacing one bearing wall with a colonnade, the architect realized an axial order that creates a simply grand organization of space. By developing the backyard, he realized a point of arrival at the end of the axis, and by removing the back wall, he made it possible for the backyard to be fully possessed by the new kitchen.*

Photos and line drawings by the architect

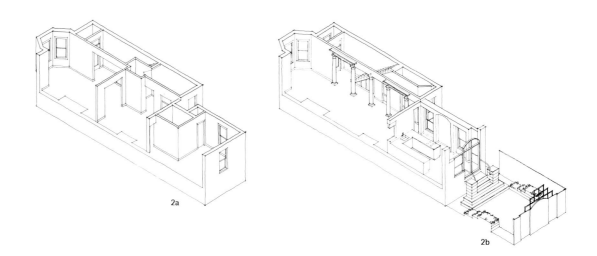

2a

2b

fig. 3 *The axis. New columns with decorative lintels and appointments replace a bearing wall. Aligning with the north wall of the kitchen, a structural cross axis occurs where the circulation path breaks to access the kitchen. Color allows certain walls to recede while emphasizing shapes. Note how the newly created recess in the far right view of the north kitchen wall creates in-wall piers following the rhythms of the new colonnade.*

fig. 4 *Garden doors. The reward at the end of the entry sequence, this new void in the brick structure (shown with doors open) focuses attention out and up. The cruciform intersection of window and door casings resting under an arched opening both centers and raises the outdoor vista. The concurrently centered back wall and planter serve as a final recognition of the power of the axis created by McInturff.*

fig. 5 *Kitchen interior. Seen through a reused opening in the lone remaining interior wall, the far side of the galley kitchen is along the circulation axis. A self-venting range minimizes appliance intrusion into the newly created space, and 4 × 4 inch tiles serve as the work surface. Note how dark color is used to define wall shapes.*

5

Extruded Gothic

A rectory kitchen is revitalized.

When the Rev. Paul F. M. Zahl married a young couple in New York City, he had fond thoughts for them both but little hope of maintaining contact let alone deepening budding friendships. The couple would settle in Connecticut, and Paul and Mary Zahl would have their ministry in some as yet unknown area.

Good intentions can lead to sporadic contact, but it was structural rot that brought the two couples together.

Paul and Mary Zahl and two (soon to be three) children began their new ministry at St. Mary's Church in Scarborough, New York. The church and rectory were quite impressive, both hewn in stone and slate in the bucolic rural style of presuburban Westchester County.

It would have been embarrassing to express it at the time, but the kitchen was as disappointing to the Zahls as the new ministry was promising. The house was designed in 1932 with a bachelor rector in mind, and the 200 square feet for cooking and eating was a disaster for a family of five, including three boys, the oldest being seven. In addition to being a functional disaster, the low-lying, flat-roofed structure seemed to be bearing the fruits of twenty years of neglect.

It was then the Zahls thought of their Connecticut couple, for the onetime groom was an architect. He also writes books about additions.

Having gotten the young architect to make a house call, the Zahls received a grim prognosis.

The kitchen structure was simply unsafe. Its Yankee-style gutters were sending most of the water that did manage to get off the kitchen's low-pitched roof into the wall cavity. Facing north, the structure really never got a chance to dry out, and rot was rampant.

CLIENTS' STATEMENT

Cooking, eating, and cleaning up in our dark kitchen were clumsy and depressing activities. As the most frequently used entry, it also collected coats, school papers, and toys. What we needed for one active young family was an entrance with storage space, a smaller, efficient kitchen work area, a separate eating area, and as much light as we could get with a north-facing room.

Within significant budget and property restrictions, we not only got what we needed but were able to include an enclosed laundry and desk as well. The result is aesthetically pleasing both inside and out, and the level of chaos has diminished considerably in the busiest area of the house.—*Paul and Mary Zahl*

As with many designs for small nonprofit groups, the architect involved had to do all his creative work without a contract or financial compensation. But it was nice to have an excuse for the couples to see each other again, and the design solution was not extremely difficult or complex.

With the same financial limitations present that prevented adequate maintenance, the architect's designs would be used to generate funding and parish commitment. Fortunately two parish members responded, one with an anonymous gift, the other with a willingness to spend most of her free time expediting the unending details involved in building an addition.

With funding in hand, the support of the parish, a favorable bid by a young contractor, and a desperate need, the work began. Because of budget limitations, the roof form over the kitchen, bounded by a steeply pitched slate roof to the south, remained a low-pitched roof, albeit more steeply pitched and drained to scuppers to prevent the chronic problems of blocked gutters and leaders.

To relieve the sense of spatial squeeze a 7-foot ceiling imposes, the architect created a large window array facing a private view and a celebratory mudroom-entry space.

A flat roof imposed on an archaic style of architecture is awkward at best. To obscure the flat-roof area of the kitchen from public view and provide a welcoming gesture, the architect created a slightly symbolic suburban Gothic form as the air lock, mudroom, and entry to the kitchen.

In so doing, the architect has solved several problems. First, space is provided for three muddy boys to hose down prior to entering the kitchen. Second, the space serves as a winter air lock and summer flue. Formally, the vertical mass announces entry to the outside world. Spatially, the ca-

1

fig. 1 *View from the south. The existing building seems to spawn a semidetached entrance. Note how the existing masonry steps down as the stucco surface treatment becomes dominant to the rear. Note also how the new mudroom roof duplicates the existing roof in material and detailing.*

fig. 2 *A gaggle of gables. Identical angles, detailing, materials, and windows create an overt linkage between the existing garage and dormer gables and the new mudroom form. Note how the simplification of the addition's detailing provides a subtle distinction between the old and the new.*

Photos by Robert Perron

2

3

4

5

fig. 3 *The kitchen. With storage wall (left), food-preparation galley (right), dining area (foreground), and mudroom (beyond door), the addition contains the classic functional components of the eat-in kitchen. Note the teak counters and laminated cabinets and the similarly detailed range hood cover in the right background.*

fig. 4 *Mudroom. The new room serves as a transitional space upon entry and as a spatial release from the low kitchen ceiling upon exit. Note the reuse of the existing lead-glass window. Note also the quarry-tile floor and the maximum-depth closet.*

fig. 5 *North wall. An enlarged window array provides light and spatial relief from a low ceiling. Note the desk to the left.*

thedralized area, naturally lit through clerestory windows, releases the squeeze of the kitchen at the end of the newly created circulation axis for those leaving; for those arriving, the peaked ceiling serves as an effective transition space.

In terms of detailing, the new roof pitch, stucco walls, slate roof, copper flashing, and salvaged leaded-glass clerestory windows all duplicate existing conditions, while the vertical mass, simplified banding, and glass doors employed key a lightly revisionist touch.

In plan, a galley kitchen condensed the cooking functions, while deep wall storage organized along the north wall and an additional 50 square feet created enough open space to accommodate a separate informal dining area. An existing stair wall was made a low wall, further increasing the visual space.

Through a great deal of nuts-and-bolts hard work, a small team, including the Zahls, the architect, the contractor, the sexton, and parish members, achieved a permanent modernization of the kitchen space at an affordable price. But more, their recognition of the problem of the potential danger of the decay and rot to the existing building enabled quick action.

When architects speak of a "forever solution," they speak of materials and details that prevent the need for excessive maintenance and a design that precludes problems from happening. Here, however, a secondary layer of intention helped create an applied forever design that, while deferential to the antique style that surrounds it, is still comfortable with its contemporary and future image.

High-Energy Addition

Solar orientation and functional utility combine in Mark Isaacs' design for a new family room in Kentucky.

PROJECT PROFILE

Owen residence
Location: Louisville, Ky.
Architect: Mark Isaacs,
Energy-Efficient Architectural
Design
Budget: $53,000
Area renovated: 1000 ft²
(including attic and office)
Area added: 400 ft²

The word "Kentucky" is not synonymous with the word "cold," but Phyllis and Tom Owen and their children spent many winter nights huddled around their fireplace.

Eventually the growing size of their children and heating bills forced the Owens to look at their seventy-year-old home with an eye toward revision. The indignity of keeping the thermostat at a constant 58°F was compounded by the cramped and dimly lit kitchen that the family occupied most hours of the day.

All of this dissatisfaction was complicated by a love of their existing home's lines and materials, not to mention a modest building budget.

With so many frustrations the Owens decided to clarify their perspective by hiring an architect. Fortunately, they found an enthusiastic practitioner of passive solar design, Mark Isaacs of Louisville, Kentucky.

Isaacs quickly pointed out to the Owens the happy circumstance of the existing rear yard's southern exposure. With the formal street side of their house facing north, the southern back of the house could be opened up to the winter sunlight and altered to accept the added square footage the Owens needed. With both backyard privacy and the formal dignity of the street facade maintained, the architect could concentrate on the potentials presented rather than the limitations imposed by the existing conditions encountered.

The existing house form was essentially a simple rectangular plan capped with a massive gambrel roof. Such a balanced and static form cannot be subtly added onto or extended. The danger of adding onto such a volume is twofold. If the architect tries to duplicate the existing scale, the addition becomes a bloated and massive form. On the other hand, if the architect tries to deny the original structure and create a semi-independent architectural event, the result

OWNER'S STATEMENT

Each year it cost more and more to heat our drafty seventy-year-old house. Our living room—especially near the fireplace in the winter—was a cluttered scene where homework, school projects, music lessons, newspaper reading, television viewing, and even informal dining were done. Our kitchen was cold in the winter and hot in the summer, with no natural light.

Our warm, new room is now the center of many of the activities earlier found in the living room. In addition, we hope that the wood-burning stove, the winter sun through south-facing glass, and the heavy insulation—aided with a few gizmos to move heat around the house—will reduce our utility bills. —*Tom Owen*

ARCHITECT'S STATEMENT

Working on the Owen house involved no mere addition. We completely restructured an older home to meet the needs of a contemporary lifestyle. My purpose in bringing about a renewed home was to produce an architecture of repose that relates very carefully to the character of the existing house and the canopy of tall trees around it. The gable—the ultimate expression of home—was the perfect form to enclose the new family room. We introduced some new spatial experiences—large connecting volumes, long interior views—and some well-crafted details in oak and tile to pull them all together. The house is now open to exterior light and view and open enough within itself to create new family-oriented spaces yet closed enough to provide a sense of protective comfort from the elements and to provide enough privacy for individual activities.

Increased thermal comfort and the probability of lower energy bills are added pluses of the Owen house renewal. —*Mark Isaacs*

can be a comical David and Goliath duet of discordant forms and rhythms.

By extending existing roof planes and surface materials, Isaacs integrated his innovations into the existing context without sacrificing his addition's formal identity.

Functionally the house that worked in 1913 was simply bereft of the informal living space that has become an essential component of a home for the 1980s. The added space could also provide some unexpected aesthetic and environmental benefits.

A typical home built in the early part of this century was designed as a subdivision of spaces within the simple volume described earlier. Isaacs realized that his new family room could spatially and visually connect those once discrete spaces. Also, the southern orientation and double height of the space added facilitate the distribution of solar-heated air into the second-story spaces. Isaacs employed generous roof overhangs and operable windows to prevent summertime overheating.

Isaacs further enhanced his energy-conscious design by utilizing 2 × 6 inch studs—increasing the depth of the insulation beyond the standard 4-inch wall cavity. Secondly, the architect employed ceiling fans, a woodstove and a rooftop strip of south-facing glazing to further reduce the energy load of the work done.

As with any truly successful design, Mark Isaacs' solution had a favorable impact on the entire house he encountered. Phyllis Owen's office gained light and space, the children's bedrooms were enlarged, and the heating bills actually may be *lowered* by the added space. All of these benefits were merely secondary amenities facilitated by the basic criteria for expansion—the addition of a family room. A simple de-congestion has delivered extraordinary by-products of aesthetic expression and environmental utility.

fig. 1 *Addition. A new back door and family room face the sun. The kinetic array of windows and trim elements activates the addition's form.*

1

fig. 2 *Exterior. The existing gambrel roof extension provides the basis for a simple gabled addition facing south. With the extension of surface materials as well as geometries, an integrated form can emerge from the existing house with harmonious results. Note the ridge extension at the roof peak bringing light into a previously unusable attic.*

2

fig. 3 *Addition elevation. A locally symmetrical array of progressive window and molding sizes. Substantial roof overhangs and a cantilevered sun screen prevent summer overheating. Note the piers at the base of the photo, an economical foundation solution.*

fig. 4 *Addition interior. With the extension of the kitchen space to the south and the removal of the existing exterior wall, a southerly facing window wall brings light and solar heating into the entire house interior. Note the open framing at the top of the photo, a remnant of the old wall structure. Note also the custom half-round fixed window at the apex of the gabled interior space.*

Photos courtesy of the architect

BEDROOMS AND BATHS

When children numerically or physically outgrow
present accommodations or when parents
financially outgrow the need for spatial
and spiritual limitations, additions
can ease the squeeze.

INTRODUCTION

There is a neat division when it comes to describing bedrooms in the American home. There is the Master Bedroom and there are all the others—for children, guests, or relatives—in subdominant postures.

Very often the "starter home" can become *the* home for a family. Moving destroys friendships children have spent young lives building, and the costs of larger homes are prohibitive, especially with college a menacing specter to financially stretched parents. Obviously homes for 2½ people cannot adequately house 4 or 5 without expansion.

The need to accommodate children and relatives is a direct spatial need brought on by increased numbers of people. The master bedroom addition is only effected in the case of the home owner reaching a state of success where money is available to provide expression of formerly repressed desires.

The needs of the two bedroom types are different and yet related; privacy and personal scale are crucial, but whereas the master bedroom is elegant, the child's bedroom best be durable. Similarly, whereas the master bath has become the vehicle for luxurious self-indulgence, the priority for the children's bath is cleanability.

The beds in master bedrooms are altars to love and are often the aesthetic fulcrum of the space; children's beds are a necessity in a room never big enough to avoid the functional and physical congestion of childhood activities. It is the master bedroom that has been infused with an unrepressed spirit in the contemporary additions in America. It is the child's bedroom that has been the subject of playful ingenuity.

Both have ceased to be simple spaces conveniently laid out above a given first-floor footprint. It can be said that an architect expresses a synthesis of spirit and form, and the variations of expression can be wonderfully realized within the simple physical accommodation of sleep.

Backyard Bonus

During a renovation, owners of a Chicago town house decide to give themselves a break.

PROJECT PROFILE

D'Alessandro residence
Location: Chicago, Ill.
Architects: Zar & Hicks
Budget: $15,000 (Phase II only)
Area renovated: None
Area added: 378 ft^2

Judy and Frank D'Alessandro had finally reached the point where they could assume full occupancy of their Chicago town house. Previously they had generated income by renting out their first floor. Now, at last, success enabled the D'Alessandros to do the painstaking renovation of their home's Victorian detailing they had dreamed of.

Fortunately, available money met immediate need, for their young sons, Josh and Mac, were approaching the double-digit age bracket that often spells the end of sharing.

So it was with one eye toward a Victorian renaissance and the other toward maintaining sibling amity that Frank and Judy D'Alessandro called Zar & Hicks, architects based in Chicago.

Given the time and money needed to undertake the overhaul of a 2700-square-foot, 100-year-old house, the D'Alessandros stressed the immediate need to remove all evidence of their downstairs apartment and accommodate two growing boys. As an aside to their young architects, they mentioned that someday, when time and money would once again allow, they might consider making their own bedroom something more than a functional accommodation.

In the best spirit of eager architects, Angela Maria Zar and Bill Hicks went to their boards and conceived a Phase II addition, focused solely on the new master bedroom and rear entry.

Two factors altered the anticipated phasing. Originally, the existing rear porch was to be repaired and reused, but when it came time to address the actual work, it became evident that time and dry rot wait for no one. Rather than spend wasted hours pouring money into a lost cause, a good stiff push was requested, and the existing back porch was almost instantly transformed into a heap of rotting wood.

OWNERS' STATEMENT

Before the renovation we lived in the second-floor apartment and rented out the first-floor apartment. When we decided to renovate the building into a single-family residence, our space-reorganization goals included providing space for an adult retreat from the world.

The addition to the rear of the building became our adult retreat. It provides us with a bedroom, bath, study, and outside deck. The stair that wraps around the exterior addition provides access to the yard and garage.

The addition created a sculptural form to the rear of the building. At night the addition resembles a Halloween pumpkin with a candle burning inside. —*The D'Alessandros*

ARCHITECT'S STATEMENT

This commission had the following criteria:
1. Create a new addition (in place of a deteriorated enclosed porch) that would expand living space.
2. Use the existing foundation for structural support of the addition.

The solutions to the problems were as follows:
1. The second floor of the addition provided a private outdoor deck and indoor study and storage area off the master bedroom. The first floor of the addition provided storage and access to the basement.
2. The semicircular roof structure of the study was an extension of the barrel-vault ceiling of the second-floor hall.
3. The second-floor exit stair was wrapped around the enclosed portion of the addition.

—*Zar & Hicks*

Fortunately, concrete footings are a bit more resistant to the onslaught of hungry bacteria, which brings us to the second reason the neatly planned phasing was quickly forgotten. For an architect's success, resourcefulness is more important than the drafting pencil. Zar and Hicks used a structural failure to argue favorably for the most cost-effective option possible: an accelerated implementation of Phase II.

Since the first floor needed access to the rear yard, *something* had to replace the dearly departed back porch. Reusing the untouched and sound foundation piers would save money, and building once is always cheaper than building twice. So rather than wait to phase in their second phase, the D'Alessandros decided to put their inhibitions behind them and build their future retreat immediately. Zar and Hicks fitted their vision to the available foundation and existing openings and created a playful addendum to a serious project.

Whereas the interior renovation of Phase I was an act of meticulous care and excruciating decisions about what is important and what is not, the addition, unseen from the street and disintegral to the existing building, could be a bit less restrained.

Several functions were accommodated by the new rear addition. First, "a secondary means of egress" for the upstairs was provided to meet the fire code. Second, access to the basement and first floor from the rear yard, which was essential, was provided. But it is the last design criterion that was addressed that made the project something special—the enrichment of the master bedroom with the addition of a study, some closets, and a deck.

Victorian bedrooms were designed to have clothing stored in armoires. The row houses seldom if ever had decks off bedrooms or curving ceilings with clerestory windows.

fig. 1 *The form. A tower form springing a horizontal extension and wrapped with a lightly simple stair. Note that the corner detailing indicates the location of the existing foundation piers.*

1

fig. 2 *Study and storage. It does not take much space to create a retreat.*

fig. 3 *The elevation. The curving top is revealed to be a circle segment, broken at the edges, duplicating the proportion of the door opening at right. Plywood, trim, and glazing take the roles of plane, line, and void respectively in this lightly kinetic facade.*

fig. 4 *The master bath isn't part of the addition itself but is a good example of high-quality fixtures and good craftsmanship creating an inviting space.*

fig. 5 *Bedroom extension. A small study and deck create a touch of spatial variety for the master bedroom. Note the curved roof.*

Photos by Fred Leavitt

2

3

4

5

Since the purpose of this addition was so antithetical to the restoration process consuming the rest of the house, the form could afford to be a bit sculptural. And since the reused foundation piers could only support wood-frame construction, the realized addition would in effect be its own building, made distinct by materials, function, construction, and detailing.

The form reflects these distinctive qualities. Essentially a tower with a rounded roof and extended wing, the addition has been designed to elicit a sense of movement and growth. Wrapping around the form is a simple stair leading to the second floor. The skin is painted; the siding is made of scored plywood with its shadow lines oriented horizontally in contrast to the vertical trim indicating the structural basis of the addition. The curved roof reflects an interior ceiling curve. A small deck and den serve the bedroom on the second floor.

In short this is an overtly new addition, standing proud of the brick facade, using surface treatments to latently express the existing pier foundation while formally doing its kinetic best to reject any allusion to the traditional back-porch form.

A minor-league phoenix, this small addition rose from the rubble to express a freedom of form inconceivable during the time of the original building's construction. Like a slightly bizarre liqueur after a large and weighty meal, this addition offers a bit of unexpected surprise and innocent assertiveness against the blank wall of the existing building.

What a pleasant bonus for a hardworking family.

The Height of Luxury

*Cass & Pinnell crown a tower with
an extraordinary bath.*

PROJECT PROFILE

West residence
Location: Washington, D.C.
Architects: Cass & Pinnell
Budget: Not available
Area renovated: 600 ft²
Area added: 600 ft² (interior)
300 ft² (deck)

What makes a bedroom and bath a master bedroom suite? Is it simply size or the inclusion of optional equipment (such as saunas, hot tubs, etc.)?

In the thick of designing an addition for a couple in Washington, D.C., Cass and Pinnell began to ask themselves that question.

Mary Beth and Rick West wanted to make their house functional by performing the now-classic renovation-addition of the kitchen, informal dining area, and deck. They had planned to simply refit the existing master bath with new fixtures, but the drawings that were flashed in front of their eyes by the architects emboldened their spirit.

If the house could support a wholly new kitchen and have decks built down to the ground, why couldn't the addition go *up* as well? The architects were enthusiastic in their suggestion that a vertical addition would best focus attention outside and serve the Wests' needs.

The implications of this choice are numerous, but one simple fact dominates all others. Without the second-story bath, there would be no tower, and without the tower, the resulting addition just would not have the magnetic and inspirational impact it now has.

The formal question decided in favor of the vertical dimension, the first question may be asked again. What does make a master bedroom suite?

A good answer might be scale. Areas such as closets or a place to dress or items such as a toilet or chest of drawers become rooms in a master bedroom suite, and they do just that in the West addition.

Another good answer might be separation. Privacy can simply mean a closed door, or in the case of a master bedroom and bath, it can mean several doors and several rooms all separate from each other and all serving to separate the bedchamber from the rest of the house. This is also designed into the West addition.

OWNERS' STATEMENT

In our addition-renovation we wanted a larger kitchen and master bath that were warm and light-filled and a deck that would integrate the house with a steeply sloping backyard.

Rather than renovating the existing master bath, we ultimately opted for building a new master bath over a portion of the new kitchen. Red oak was used for the floors, the walls, and cathedral ceiling, and it added tremendous warmth to the room. The Jacuzzi we included in the plans was placed in front of a large bay window that provided both light and a sweeping yet private view of treetops and the parklands that are located behind our property.

Conceding that our construction was an addition, we nevertheless wanted it to look as little like an addition as possible.
—*Rick and Mary Beth West*

ARCHITECTS' STATEMENT

Rick and Mary Beth West's pre-World War II brick house is set on a sloping and wooded site overlooking a branch of Washington's Rock Creek Park. When the Wests came to us, their house suffered from most of the complaints heard about structures of that vintage in attractive locations; it had a tiny kitchen, no informal family-use area (they have two young children), and an inadequate master bedroom and bath. In addition, the house made very little use of the yard and views.

We opened the master suite out toward the view, added a new master bath, converted a small bedroom across the center hall into a dressing room, and connected the three, which make up the addition's second level, with a back passage.

We tried to make the *character* of the addition to match what it was intended to do—give the Wests new rooms that bridged between the house and its site.—*Cass & Pinnell*

Yet another criterion for a master bedroom suite might be finish. Whereas formica and wall-to-wall carpeting are standard in bedrooms and baths, the master bedroom suite luxuriates in hardwoods, tile, wainscoting—all are very well evidenced in the West addition.

But what of bathroom equipment or cathedral ceilings or custom millwork? They are all, indeed, a part of the West addition.

What is present in the West addition's approach to the master bath and plan reorganization of the existing house is almost the prototype of a couple's plunge into a little self-indulgence.

First of all, the existing plan gave over one bedroom to the cause of adequate closet space. Second, a wall was added to connect all distinct parts of the suite without contact with the house, creating the needed separation.

With the addition of a separate bath that combined not only all the plumbing prerequisites but the finish, detailing, and spatial qualities of a master bath, the project presents a maximum amount of functional luxury per square foot.

The essential truth about this particular project is that the actual bedroom was quite adequate, but the ancillary spaces were either inadequate or nonexistent. Perhaps that is what makes a designed space so different from one that is simply constructed. The act of design questions the needs of the occupants and responds with built form. The act of unthinking construction builds a space that the occupants then have to question and adapt to.

In creating a master bedroom and bath, the essential concern is not luxury but comfort. In its compact arrangement and custom quality, the West master bath enables utility and efficiency to provide true comfort for the Wests.

In a very real sense, the components added by Cass and Pinnell have transformed the Wests' bedroom without even touching it.

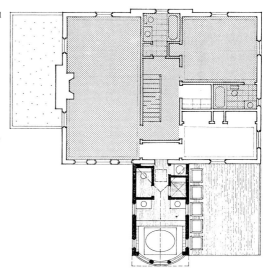

fig. 1 *Bath plan. By adding a bathroom (dark lines) and renovating part of the existing plan (white area), the architects turn a bedroom (left side of plan) into a master bedroom.*

fig. 2 *An extraordinary exterior form. Horizontal shadow lines are broken only by the imposed two-story tower element enclosing dining area and master bath. Note that the shingling at the roof pediment matches the existing second-floor finish. The forms of the deck and kitchen (right) components seem to be in supportive deference to the noble tower.*

Line drawing by the architects
Photos by Arnold Kramer

fig. 3 *Kitchen. Not the focus of this article, the kitchen and its adjacent dining area are nonetheless the spatial horizontal plinth for the new bathroom's vertical endeavors.*

fig. 4 *Looking back. Double sinks, illuminated by lighting on pediments, serve as end pieces for the condensed toilet and shower rooms. The entire interior skin is in oak, allowing the internal constructions to read as sculpted objects. Note the south-facing chamfered corner and skylight in upper center.*

fig. 5 *(Opposite) The tub. This is virtually the cockpit for the entire addition. The architects have allowed for modesty by determining from sight-line analysis that no one can see in. Note the tile molding at the ceiling break point; note also the built-in side lighting of the Jacuzzi platform. The multiple round windows repeat a motif that can be seen in the kitchen interior.*

Bay Duet

Louis Mackall creates a master bedroom with a minimum of means.

PROJECT PROFILE

Howland residence
Location: Greenwich, Conn.
Architect: Louis Mackall,
Louis Mackall & Partner
Budget: $20,000
Area renovated: 200 ft²
Area added: 60 ft²

Martha and Bill Howland owned a home of mixed legacies. Originally, two cottages were built in the nineteenth century and later were combined to create one house. The results were too many stairs, too few bathrooms, small closets, and, most discouraging of all, no discernible master bedroom amid the jumble of rooms on the second floor.

The Howlands lived with these inconveniences until the children just became too old to continue split shifts of shared bathroom use. They called in Louis Mackall, an architect adept at making buildings more civilized.

The program was classic: to provide a bathroom of their own, more space, more closets, and, distinctively enough, a setting for a marvelous nineteenth-century sleigh bed.

Mackall perceived the problem on another level as well. In all the rush to combine the two cottages way back when, something had gotten lost in the transition—any recognition of the front door.

Without this perceived need, the solution would have been simple—extend enough space over the existing porch to accommodate the new functions desired. But the Howlands hired Mackall to make something beautiful as well as useful, and the final solution, which is so simple, belies the hours of work required to knit exterior form and interior utility into a unified whole.

Some extension over the porch was called for, and some space could be pirated from adjacent children's rooms. But the key to overcoming the physically limited area for expansion lay in the way the new interior space was perceived.

The crucial generating signal was present in the existing bay window tucked under the third-floor gable. Mackall saw that by applying its angled geometries, an entire

OWNER'S STATEMENT

The objective was to add a bathroom to the master bedroom while preserving the character of the house. We felt we could not get space without interfacing with the lines of the house.

The results of the project were:

1. Useful space in the bathroom and bedroom
2. Openness, including light, cross ventilation, and views that we did not have before
3. Enhanced exterior design
4. Placement of the bed on the outside wall so that we can see out with a 200° sweep of view

—*Martha Howland*

ARCHITECT'S STATEMENT

The Howland addition was designed and built to solve two problems. The first was the clients' need for a larger bedroom and an extra bathroom, the second was an existing exterior that reminded me of the face of a prizefighter who had lost too many fights. If you will look at the before photograph, you will see that his nose is pushed off to one side and that the column below can't decide whether the nose or the forehead is its rightful owner. A hundred drawings later we have brought the various parts of the face together again.

The issue is the same with any addition: how to get the most for the least. The rule is to magnify the strengths and minimize the weaknesses. The method is to bring fresh eyes every time and remember that there are a thousand good solutions.—*Louis Mackall*

bay window wall could extend over the porch and provide a perfect perch for the thoroughly grand sleigh bed.

With the bed pushed south, the new bath could be nestled north, and closets could be placed to the west.

The new bay would center on the existing gambrel gable. In a perfect example of unrelated design, the spacing of the front-porch columns had no orientation to this centering peak. One column came within a foot of the gambrel bay's center, so by adding another column, Mackall created a paired vertical element recognizing the centerline and, by sheer luck, announcing the location of the front door opposite it.

The bay extension faced south, and Mackall used his extended bay to create a clerestory fan window, breaking the low ceiling plane above the Howlands' sleeping heads.

Secondarily, there was a view that the bedroom never had a chance to recognize—a nearby pond. Mackall further utilized his bay window geometry and extended the angled east side of the bed bay beyond the existing wall plane several feet and returned it back to the building to create a second bay, literally pointing the way to the view.

Two by-product benefits from this second extension were realized. A means for cross ventilation was created, and unexpectedly, the new angled extension could be used structurally.

When work began, it was assumed by all parties that the porch roof was a sound structure. After all, half of the existing bedroom depended on it. But when the building's skin was removed, there was almost nothing under it to keep the floor from simply collapsing. The floor was reframed, and the angled bay provided a needed extension from which an independent column

1

fig. 1 *The realized scheme. A newly prominent bay proudly extends from under the gambrel roof. The semicircular window, the only curved form in the house, further focuses attention. The newly formed "face" to the street is fully fleshed out and made symmetrical by doubling the columns beneath the new bay.*

fig. 2 *Existing house. A modest bay window nestles beneath a gambrel roof overhang. Note the disintegration of the gambrel form, middle bay, and front porch.*

Photos by Robert Perron

2

fig. 3 *The second bay. Facing a backyard pond, the second bay is a simple extension of one side facet of the primary bay. Note the column, which bypasses the structural load, away from the inadequate porch framing below the new bay.*

fig. 4 *The second-bay interior. Breaking the confines of the existing house, the minor bay faces a previously unappreciated backyard view. To the left, the new bath is located for ease of access; note the angled access corner minimizing the room's imposition on the sleeping area.*

fig. 5 *The main-bay interior. Note the raised ceiling to accommodate the new southerly glazing and the magnificent sleigh bed around which the addition is designed.*

fig. 6 *Bath. Mirror, Corian, and sandblasted glass create a bath that is both highly sophisticated and custom-crafted. Note the use of wall-to-wall mirror to visually enlarge the small space, incorporating the medicine cabinet within its plane.*

could be dropped for support. Aesthetically it was more of an animated appendage than a column, but it did the job nonetheless.

On the interior, Mackall let the bed dominate the bedroom, but in the bath, Martha Howland knew what she wanted. A material called Corian has all the sensual properties of marble but can be cut and shaped like wood. Martha Howland asked Mackall and his other business, Breakfast Woodworks, to give her a Corian bathroom. They jumped at the chance.

The standard vanity top of Corian with sink sprung a shelf, which in turn sprung a towel bar, which in turn sprung a toilet-paper holder—all under the careful touch of Mackall and his woodworking company.

The material was reused in conjunction with the glass door fronts, mirrored vanity, and shower stall to create a harmony of flat grainless surfaces.

Louis Mackall did not simply solve the given problem, he solved *all* the problems he could perceive. In so doing, an architect becomes more than a problem-solving practitioner, he becomes an architectural therapist, willing to go to extra lengths both to discover hidden dilemmas and create solutions.

In this particular case, views were recognized as important, a floor was saved from collapse, a material was integrated in innovative ways, the bed was given a stage to strut, and perhaps most importantly, a blank facade was given a warmly inviting visage. All of this and 60 additional square feet, too!

Sanctuary

A dormer turns unusable attic space into a spiritual haven.

PROJECT PROFILE

Greenberg residence
Location: New Haven, Conn.
Architects: Ben Benedict and
Carl Pucci, BumpZoid
Budget: $4000 (1975)
Area renovated: 200 ft^2
Area added: 15 ft^2

Although their house was quite large by any standard, the home owned by Stanley Greenberg and his wife was definitely not big enough for the two of them. Their marriage was rapidly becoming untenable, and the emotional discord they felt needed physical separation to make their lives livable. So a new bedroom had to be found, and the attic seemed both remote and spacious enough.

Fortunately Stanley Greenberg, a Yale professor, had heard of two young graduates who went around New Haven designing and building little parts onto old buildings. Although these "boys" have since taken to wearing suits and calling themselves BumpZoid, Ben Benedict and Carl Pucci were as ingenious back in the mid-1970s as they are now.

When the couple called them in to look at their attic, the young designer-builders knew that the only way art would be served by these unhappy circumstances would be if they could "put on a happy face" architecturally.

A poet might say a dormer is a dormer is a dormer, but Pucci and Benedict tried their energetic best to translate a pressing need and a slim budget into a positive statement.

Simply, the dormer used the high existing roof peak to create a clerestory space. The dormer itself was a bit more complex than the standard gable version. Necking down at the clerestory window, the form was just atypical enough to support being made even more abnormal. This was accomplished by applying a Renaissance- or Flemish-outlined false front.

The visual effect was that of a facade extension slicing through the roof much in the way the now-legendary tab A is inserted into slot B.

The interior is simply a billowing ceiling of gypsum wallboard following the roof rafters, with the exposed rough-hewn tie beams serving as counterpoint.

Every cloud has its silver lining. Though the Greenbergs divorced, the dormer remains. And even though Ben Benedict and Carl Pucci now practice architecture on Fifth Avenue in New York City, their venturesome hearts still find delight in doing a small job well.

OWNER'S STATEMENT

The purpose of the project was to allow a livable space in an attic that was otherwise only suitable for storage. In fact, the renovations were made necessary by an impending separation and the need to keep irreconcilable people in the same house.

Ben and Carl presented a model that was in response to our request for a dormer. Our initial reaction was horror, and my ex-wife insisted to the end that the new roof had no business atop our house. Ben and Carl would not consider any compromise on the model, and we proceeded on faith.

I ultimately decided to accept the plan because the dormer looked vaguely like the Cape Dutch architecture of South Africa. Since my academic specialty took me regularly to South Africa, I thought it would make a nice addition. At no time had I communicated this interest to Ben and Carl and cannot imagine how they settled on this approach.

Ben and Carl performed all the work, excepting plumbing and electrical work. Even on these jobs, however, they regularly refigured the work of specialists, improving design and saving money.

—Stanley B. Greenberg

ARCHITECT'S STATEMENT

Light
Aer
Divorce
Illusion
Allusion

—Ben Benedict

fig. 1 *Inside. Beams and plants fill a rather high volume of space. The limits of an attic space are eliminated by going so far up as well as out. Note the leather restraints across the French doors cum casement windows.*

fig. 2 *The house. Covered in the same siding, the new dormer is just lofty enough to become a single large ornament for the house as a whole.*

fig. 3 *The dormer. Doors become very large casement windows as a similarly outsized transom pushes the facade up. Note that the corners are the only false portion of the facade.*

Photos by Robert Perron

2

3

1

Their Own World

*Confronted with shrinking space and privacy,
a New Haven couple seek refuge in their attic.*

PROJECT PROFILE

Ross residence
Location: New Haven, Conn.
Architects: Ben Benedict and
Carl Pucci, BumpZoid
Budget: $60,000
Area renovated: 600 ft²
Area added: 100 ft²
(under dormers)

Carol and Steve Ross needed some peace and quiet. They loved to read and work together in a tranquility that was becoming harder and harder to find as their children grew bigger and bigger.

Normally when children reach a certain age, they demand their own territory, their "space." Parents, eager to isolate bad habits, often convert a garage or renovate an attic, where the adolescents in question can claim supremacy.

In this instance, the parents felt besieged by the growing mutual impositions and pinched by the lack of space readily at hand. In response they called two architects who had renovated their kitchen several years earlier: BumpZoid, alias Carl Pucci and Ben Benedict. It became clear the only way to expand was up. Thinking it over, the Rosses decided that stars over your head made a lot less noise than not-so-tiny-little feet. The decision was made to create a parents' floor for work and leisure.

With their space staked out, Pucci and Benedict started from scratch. An existing bath and stair would have to stay in their locations for budgetary reasons. Similarly, the somewhat low roof could be broken by dormers but could not be raised as a whole.

BumpZoid proceeded to take what the budget and home would give. The cheapest way to gain volume in an attic is to reach into the space at the peak of the ceiling. Since the roof had a single ridge line, an axis was determined. Since both the bath and stair were located at one end of the plan, the bed was pushed to the farthest corner away from their imposition and conversely the work area was oriented toward the stair.

The plan designed itself by straightforward zoning criteria. The linking ceiling axis connected the public end (terminated by the stair) to the private end (terminated by the sleeping area). As with all successful axial plans, the endpoints needed excitement and the axis itself needed a cross axis to enliven the obvious linearity. Given the low level of the roof, dormers were the obvious method of gaining light and space.

To allow for a pleasant sleeping environment, the bed claimed a dormer. To create the cross axis mentioned, an opposing dormer served the dressing area. Since the existing stair lacked adequate headroom for full-time use, the ceiling needed to be raised at this point—and since this was at the major axial terminus, a pyramidal skylight was placed on top of the new dormer incorporating the stair.

None of these planning moves described displays extraordinary insight or exceptional mental gymnastics, but there is quiet brilliance in the way BumpZoid developed these elements into a series of distinct parts all relating to the dominant axis defined at the roof peak.

The axis itself is a case in point. When a ceiling is to be raised, the underside of the rafters provides a convenient plane of attachment for the applied gypsum wallboard, hence the now-hackneyed cathedral ceiling. Pucci and Benedict realized that a simplistic peak was a visual dead end. To invigorate their axis, they used a stepped, or corbeled, interior trough of space seemingly carved out of the attic ceiling. Whereas a cathedral ceiling has space, this overt axis has depth and a form of its own.

Similarly, a dormer can be framed to support a little interior cathedral or framed for a flat ceiling. With the bedroom-area dormers cutting out broad sections of roof, major ceremonial spaces could have been inserted. Instead, Benedict and Pucci knew that the axis was the dominant spatial delineator, hence the interior form of the dormers became a soft underbelly curve, embracing the bed and becoming its headboard.

OWNER'S STATEMENT

Ben Benedict and Carl Pucci of BumpZoid renovated our kitchen. When we decided to renovate our third floor, making it into an area in which Carol and I could work and sleep, we called them.

The third floor had a bathroom, a small bedroom, and an unfinished play area. We wanted a large bedroom, bathroom, and area to work. We insisted upon ample storage and sufficient bookcases for our large library. We also wanted natural light and a good view of our yard. While we didn't want the third floor to be a play area for the children, we did want them to feel welcome and to come up freely. But, basically, we wanted a quiet, private area to be created.

Our requirements were beautifully met. The area is light and open and is cool in the summer. The storage is plentiful. We enjoy the whimsical touches and the classical sophistication of the area.—*Steve Ross*

ARCHITECT'S STATEMENT

Axis (horizontal and vertical)
Light
Comfort
Zones
Materials
                            —*Ben Benedict*

1

fig. 1 *Exterior. An interior space becomes an exterior form. The terminal dormer becomes the focus for the entire back of the house. Capped by a copper ziggurat and skylight, the outlandish roof form sits upon a simple shape wrapped in the building's existing skin and centers above the BumpZoid-designed kitchen entrance.*

fig. 2 *Axis perspective. Low-lying dormers and discrete subspaces all derive focus and power from the ordering axis.*

Line drawing by the architects
Photos by Langdon Clay

2

fig. 3 *Minor focus. Twin doors leading to the same space create a center for the column. Corresponding light fixture serves as a positive focus. Note the bed to right.*

fig. 4 *Bed. The backwater for all the axial dynamics, the bed is locked into its space by millwork and the spatial headboard of the dormer. The gentle arch signals a safe haven. Note the stepped detailing of the bed platform and the strip of accent lights along the top of the picture.*

fig. 5 *Interior focus. Solid form is punctured, spatial flow released. Note the reveal on the first corbel riser; it houses tiny accent lights. Note also the common work area to the left.*

3

Lastly, a skylight can be a piece of hardware dropped into an existing framing pattern. Or it can be an event. Since the stepped through axis is indeed the dominant datum for the entire floor, its terminus must be expressed as a reasonable extension of the form employed. As a gesture evidencing the imposition of the axis, the corbeled interior form becomes a copper ziggurat on the exterior, capped by the pyramidal skylight.

It is in the considered imposition of incongruous elements that an architect can inexpensively change an entire context. By focusing on a slightly fantastic axis and a series of subdominant dormers, lighting fixtures, bookcases, and other millwork items, BumpZoid has made the Rosses' bedroom an adult sanctuary and a celebratory sequence of events.

4

5

A Cottage Retreat

William F. Stern creates a pavilion for sleeping in suburban Houston.

The advent of the first baby transforms a couple into a family in short order. When the owners of a rambling one-story suburban home outside of Houston, Texas, became in the family way, their thoughts turned to their existing cluster of bedrooms. Although the number of rooms was adequate to house a young family, the quality of space, storage, and privacy available rapidly became a pressing issue.

The rambling plan of the typical ranch-style home built in the 1950s offered little spatial differentiation and no vertical release from the oppressively unbroken standard 8-foot ceiling height.

When frustration with an existing house becomes pressurized by a radical change in functional requirements, the need for an architect becomes almost undeniable. The owners contacted William F. Stern in the hope that he might be able to address their changing needs and add some excitement to their undifferentiated agglomeration of rooms.

Stern found little inspiration in the house he encountered. After several consultations, he realized that the owners basically wanted a separate little house of their own linked to the existing house but not incorporated into it. Of course, the new addition had to respond to the other imminent familial addition by being located in close proximity to the baby's room. But just as a new baby requires a certain surrender of privacy, those rare moments of peace that do occur should be enhanced by the orientation and quality of the parents' only refuge, their bedroom.

Stern knew that the spirit of his work was as important as the functional criteria he had to accommodate. It became obvious to Stern that he could create a backyard ensemble of seemingly separate buildings. A courtyard could be formed by using the ex-

OWNERS' STATEMENT

We were expecting our first child when we asked William F. Stern to design a master bedroom addition to include a dressing room, bathroom, bedroom, and study. Specifically, this master suite was to be approximately 600 to 700 square feet and provide maximum privacy. In addition, Stern was advised to place emphasis on good design rather than on modern gadgetry. Months of interviews, meetings, and revisions produced a sophisticated and exciting yet simple design reflecting a subtle respect for our lifestyle. The proof of the success of the design is the overwhelming feeling of dwelling in a life-size piece of art rather than merely occupying a room.

ARCHITECT'S STATEMENT

The suburbs of Houston, particularly those developed in the 1950s, are populated chiefly by meandering one-story houses designed in the builder's vocabulary of the time. Commissioned to do a project in such a suburb, we made an early decision to build the new master bedroom suite as an architecturally designed object. The connection to the house maintains the proportion of the original structure. The bedroom then takes on an expanded volume as a relief to 8-foot ceilings throughout the rest of the house.

The roof pitches steeply, giving the addition the character of the original American cottage. The bedroom addition is white-painted board and batten, making reference to cottage construction of the nineteenth century.

It was our intention to elevate the spatial experience from both the inside and outside, by adding a surprising addendum to the rambling and otherwise anonymous builder's house.—*William F. Stern*

isting house, freestanding garage, and tree already in place and by orienting the bedroom to create the fourth side.

While the brick-faced structure sprawled to the west, the slightly more compact garage stood to the north and was sheathed in the traditional white-painted board and batten siding. Since both buildings shared the unrelentingly low eave height, Stern saw the opportunity in creating the new courtyard's architectural focus by designing something a bit more vertically inclined. The danger in asserting a new form is in creating an incongruous element that will prevent the new grouping from being perceived as an ensemble.

Stern seized upon the garage siding as his link to the existing conditions. When it was applied to a vertical form, the natural result was quite evocative of the nineteenth-century farmhouse cottages that once covered the Texas landscape.

Internally the four parts of a master bedroom suite (bathroom, closet and dressing area, sitting area, and sleeping area) were organized to maximize privacy. The new bathroom was located adjacent to an existing plumbing core, with the closet and dressing area naturally oriented in close proximity. These spaces thus became the low linkage to the existing building, creating a buffer from the adjacent bedrooms.

The "cottage" itself would contain the sitting and sleeping areas. Given the orientation of the addition toward the new courtyard, the sitting area could serve as an effective buffer from the developed exterior space.

The sleeping area that resulted was cozily nestled in a secluded corner of the house but maintained a dual accessibility to the adjacent bedrooms and the outside world. Since this cottage would be an area of repose, the ceilings were cathedralized to the

1

fig. 1 *Exterior. The "cottage" master bedroom proudly faces the newly defined exterior space. Note the existing tree to the right.*

fig. 2 *Plan. The black lines indicate the area added. Closets and bath serve as both linkage and buffer to the house, as does the sitting room in its orientation to the courtyard. The squared bay window responds to the entry axis. The newly defined exterior courtyard can be easily seen.*

Line drawing by the architect
Photos by Paul Hester

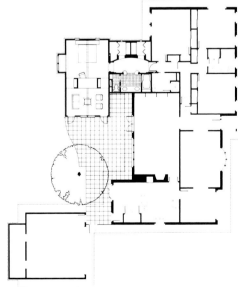

4

3

fig. 3 *Bedroom built-in desk. Bookcases and storage units provide the infill for this deep wall construction. The arched opening centers the bed-bound focus.*

fig. 4 *Bedroom. A simple space, placidly centered by the ceiling peak. The frameless window seems to puncture the end wall, providing vignettes of the outside world. Built-in cabinets (integrated throughout the entire project by the detailing) eliminate the need for additional furniture.*

fig. 5 *Bath. Finished surfaces and thoughtful detailing prevent the need for doors or furniture. The pocket door (center left) provides separation for the toilet. Built-in seats and mirror create a sense of complete design. Note the bay window axially oriented to the entrance.*

fig. 6 *Sitting area. Facing the backyard, this vertical space has direct access to the new backyard patio. The existing garage can be seen through the window. Note the celestial accent window providing a visual high point for the room.*

fig. 7 *Entry. Built-in dressers provide a finished closet interior preventing the need for doors. The bowed wall relieves the sense of corridor and focuses on the bathroom opening opposite.*

5

6

7

underside of the relatively steeply pitched new roof, catching the space often occupied by a wandering mind.

The functional divisions within the addition are segregated without doors by relying on orientation and built-in elements to define space and focus attention. The resulting flow of spaces and variety of forms encountered are unprecedented in the existing house.

The clients wanted a restful retreat and relief from their all too typical suburban home. William F. Stern provided a positive focus for the house as a whole and a celebration of a happy marriage and future family. Somehow a long-slumbering suburban house has been allowed to dream a little.

Tree House

Confronted by two massive oaks, Mark McInturff builds a bedroom tower.

PROJECT PROFILE

Miller residence
Location: Chevy Chase, Md.
Architect: Mark McInturff,
Wiebenson & McInturff, Architects
Budget: $60,000
Area renovated: 200 ft²
Area added: 450 ft²

OWNERS' STATEMENT

We were looking to add a fourth bedroom and to expand our kitchen and eating space. We had never done an addition before, and it took longer than we expected. Despite the delays (the whole process took seven months) we are very pleased with how the addition tied the back of the house together so well.

—June and Todd Miller

ARCHITECT'S STATEMENT

Our plan was to reopen the center hall through the house and to organize the rooms to either side. What made all this somewhat more difficult was the presence of two grand oak trees very close to the house directly at the end of the hall. Our new addition goes to some effort, architecturally and structurally, to wrap around these trees without doing them harm.

The center hall now arrives at a configuration of house, addition, trees, column, beams, and stairs that celebrates the weaving together of house and site. From a small second-floor balcony high above the ground, one can reach out and touch one of the trees that so determined this configuration.—Mark McInturff

June and Todd Miller had one bedroom too few and two trees too many. A growing family, the Millers needed to decongest their kitchen and add another bedroom to their suburban home in Chevy Chase, Maryland. Standing in the path of their desire to expand were two grand old oak trees, the closest of which was not 5 feet from the back of the house.

Realizing that they had to both save the trees and make their house livable, the Millers contacted Mark McInturff to resolve their seemingly mutually exclusive desires.

As with most inspired designers, McInturff saw only the opportunities provided by the oaken imposition.

The trees are quite mature, their trunks rising many feet without branches reaching out to gather in sunlight. The architect knew that no matter what he did, his addition would have to be in concert with the trees, for to confront their power or ignore it would ultimately be a waste of time and effort.

McInturff only had to look at an existing sun-room addition to see the results of arbitrary spatial imposition. Its low lean-to form fairly cringed beneath the dominant presence of the mighty oaks. McInturff took pity on the rather conventional sun room and integrated it into his new composition by aligning its painted clapboard siding and horizontal elements with those in his new addition. In so doing, he could present a unified ensemble across the entire south facade of the house. McInturff thereby created a formal scale that was necessary to respond to the twin towers embraced by the new construction.

On the first floor, the kitchen location was maintained and an informal dining area was added, roughly 12 feet square, with the southerly wall taking the form of a large bay window. In order to minimize the addition's impact on the trees' root systems, the entire load of the new structure is carried by the existing foundation wall to the north and by only two new pier footings to the south. Since the span between the supports is about 20 feet in length, a lightweight steel beam was used with the bay window floor structure cantilevering out from its line of support. Filling in the void between the new and existing additions, two small decks and connecting stairs provide access to ground level.

Although ingenious in its avoidance of the trees and responsive to the needs of the owners, this first floor would do little but serve as a simple response to what the site allowed if not for the vertical verve of the second-story bedroom. Extending from the new bay window wall below, both the form and detailing of the bedroom attempt to do many things and in fact do them all quite well.

McInturff realized that his first-floor bay window wall was not part of the existing house's vernacular of building parts. He used the second story of his addition to erode that angled massing to the point where only one proud gable element remains. The form of this element is almost identical to the dormers that were already present in the house, creating a lofty referential feature.

The first-floor steel beam mentioned before has its counterparts supporting the second floor and roof structure. Since these upper beams did not have to support the deck present on the first floor, they could be made of dimensional lumber. The simplest support solution for these upper beams would be to use the pier foundations located so carefully to avoid major disruption of the trees' root systems. The east support could be buried in the new wall, while the west support condition was oriented to the far western corner of the new deck. Rather

1

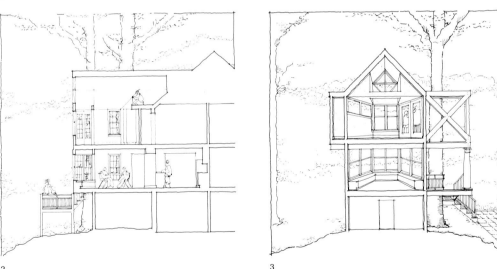

2   3

fig. 1 *South elevation. With the existing sun room to the left providing the basis for the exterior finish treatment, the tower addition rises up alongside the existing oaks. Instead of simply picking a window out of context as the existing sun-room addition had, McInturff opted to duplicate the windows already present in the original house and only violate that system at the crowning glory of his tower form, the diamond clerestory window. Note the implicit connection between the diagonal orientation of the window and the cross bracing of the expressed beaming. Note also the culminating gable's direct allusion to the existing dormer form seen in the left background of the picture.*

fig. 2 *Cutaway view at peak of addition roof. A sense of the various spaces involved can be seen in this sketch. Dark lines indicate where the building's walls are cut. The first floor is defined by the direct extension of wall and ceiling planes from the existing house. The second floor lets the tower form of the addition become a lofty space on the interior, with its own balcony.*

fig. 3 *Interior perspective. This view gives a good indication of the horizontal beaming that occurs under the first and second floors and is expressed at the roof level. Whereas the first-floor glazing is quite normal, the second floor takes the traditional window form and animates it by a progressive dropping of the sill. Note how the clerestory dormer is framed by the roof form and by the expressed beam running under it.*

Photos and line drawings by the architect

fig. 4 *Focus on the trees. By extending the existing addition's horizontal banding of siding and trim work and by aligning eaves with the existing building, the architect allows a sensible system to accept permutations (as in the tiny second-story deck or cross-bracing beaming) or eccentric impositions (such as tree trunks or a classic column). There is another level of rational expression present in the relationship between the window muntins and deck-rail detailing. In creating a light tracery of orthogonal lines, the architect makes a small-scale system dance about the large interacting forms, creating a richer combination of elements.*

fig. 5 *Bedroom clerestory dormer. The view from the loft shows the spatial ambiguity between the space at eye level, focused on the window, and the peripherally apprehended space somewhat below eye level. Note the descending windowsills, left to right, finishing in the tiny balcony in the lower right corner.*

5

than hide his structural design, McInturff chose to express his long-span beaming as an open frame extending through the west wall above the deck. This element incorporates the diagonal lines of cross bracing and sits between the two trees, forming a marvelous mesh of built and natural forms.

Obviously, exterior formal manipulations have internal spatial implications, and as with all thoughtful designs, the results in this scheme are positive. By culminating his tower form in a gable, McInturff created the clerestory light-ing that allowed a small loft to be usable space. By imposing a rectilinear geometry on the bay window form, he created a small deck at the west corner of the bedroom.

Mark McInturff took on the challenge of an awkward site and used it to the design's advantage. The Millers had all of their needs met by the addition and realized an aesthetic potential undreamed of at the outset of the project. It is in these areas of unexpected delight that architecture can have its most beneficial effect—when utility and the artistic muse combine to redefine our expectations.

Fantasy Fulfilled

*Louis Mackall & Partner create
a spectacular space.*

PROJECT PROFILE

Singer residence
Location: Riverside, Conn.
Architects: Louis Mackall and
Duo Dickinson, Louis Mackall &
Partner
Budget: $70,000 (estimate for
bedroom only)
Area renovated: None
Area added: 400 ft²

Ron and Anne Singer owned a rare commodity. They owned a Greenwich, Connecticut, home that had more acreage than it needed.

Fortunately for the Singers no one had subdivided their double lot, and their somewhat standard 1920s home had plenty of space around it. Real estate agents said the value of the house did not proportionally match their land's value; hence if they ever wanted to sell, their house would be somewhat beneath its maximum profit potential.

But resale values aside, the Singers had just run out of room. In a 10 × 20 foot sun porch, the stereo, videocassette recorder, and color television were all wedged next to a desk, which in turn was surrounded by overloaded bookcases. The kitchen had not been touched for a couple of decades, and almost as an afterthought, the Singers realized that as long as they were renovating, it would be great to have a "real" master bath, with a Jacuzzi for Ron's bad back.

With this checklist firmly in hand, they called Louis Mackall & Partner, architects. Louis and his partner, who happens to be this book's author, studied the intricate functional requirements formulated by Anne Singer and set out to thoroughly reinvent the house.

The existing building was a simple two-story house made special by using a pseudo-gambrel roof element that tried to make the second floor look like a long shed (non-peaked) dormer. The effect was intended to break down the mass of the house's essentially boxlike form.

Seeing beyond the applied roof fragments, the architects gained a measure of respect for the materials and detailing of the skin of the building; stucco and broad molding maintained a high level of quality both in design and execution.

OWNER'S STATEMENT

We wanted to make an addition to our house because we felt we were bursting at the seams. Unexpectedly, the star of the addition turned out to be the new master bedroom, located right above the family room and sharing its curved wall. The room extends so far into the branches of the giant maple tree that you almost feel as if you are living in it.

Based on our experience, we offer the following advice to prospective rebuilders:

- Before sending out the final plans for bids, make sure you check and have *all* your changes incorporated into them.
- Always communicate all your instructions directly.
- Allow for a one-third increase in the bid for changes.
- If it's supposed to take four months, allow for six.
- Be prepared for total chaos and disruption.
- Hang in there; the final result is worth it.—*Anne Singer*

ARCHITECT'S STATEMENT

The Singer bedroom is to the bedroom as Power Samba is to music. It plays upon a strong relationship between bed and wall swelling out toward the large tree in the side yard. Hot tub and elevated bathroom are placed to magnify that direction; skylights, strong over the sinks, turn to salt and pepper as they circle up toward the loft. In plan as well as detailing, the two main attributes of the space—direction and volume—are magnified. The power of that combination is received by the bed.— *Louis Mackall*

Rather than deny this best aspect of the house exterior, the architects simply extended it, creating a hemicycle terminus for the house. By animating the eave and cornice lines, the roof, and the wall planes, the architects created a continuous wrapping skin, which then could have new windows and doors seemingly cut into it.

On the first floor the sun porch was removed, since it would have been enveloped by the new extension. In its place went a large family room, taking up the entire area of the new addition. A small stair leading to the new master bedroom was inserted at the intersection of the addition and the existing house.

In their quest to decongest, the Singers saw an expanded role for their bedroom. First, Anne, who is a writer, needed to have her own place. Second, some of the home-entertainment functions could be included in the bedroom planning. Last, all of the clothing storage, which had been spread throughout the house, could be collected in this one room.

But the architects knew that whatever functions occurred, the most impressive aspect of this room would be the space defined by the half-round plan and cathedral ceiling.

It was clear that the closet and bath functions should be condensed to the back of the space, and along with the bed and desk functions these large-scale elements could form a variated landscape under the curving ceiling.

Opacity is the requisite quality for closets. Separation and proximity are the bathroom's ironic location criteria. But for the desk and the bed, view and orientation are the paramount concerns. Obviously the most special of vistas occurs in this space from the center point that generates the curving wall. So the architects created a geometri-

1   *Robert Perron*

BEFORE

AFTER

2

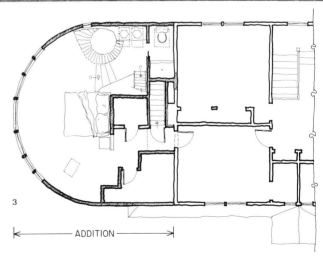

3

|← ADDITION →|

fig. 1 *Exterior. Extended eave heights, wall planes, materials, and detailings create a radical transition without disruption.*

fig. 2 *Architects' sketches. A house is transformed by the lateral extension of its existing form to create an unabashed "head" for the home.*

fig. 3 *Plan. New walls are cross-hatched. Existing walls are extended to form a hemicycle terminus to the originally gable-ended form. Two entries to the new bedroom are created by inserting a new "secret stair" (center) and appropriating an existing bedroom as a transitional sewing room and entry (lower right). Utilitarian spaces such as the bath, stair, and closets are arranged to the existing house side, allowing the bed to rest in an unencumbered space, focused on an expansive array of windows (left).*

Line drawings by the architects

4

fig. 4 *A highly civilized hot tub helps create a threshold to the open bath. Custom millwork facilitates an effortless transition from sleeping space to hygenic environment. The most personal bath functions are discreetly tucked into their own skylit room beyond the vanity. A pocket door is utilized to minimize the intrusion of a door into the several functions reaching confluence at the point of entry into this subspace. Note the use of water-resistant teak for the tub surround. Note also the built-in bedside table to the right, the custom ladder stair beyond, and the small custom window allowing an outside view to the tub dweller. It should be noted that due to the elevated floor level and continuity of eave height, the skylights provide spatial relief as well as added light.*

fig. 5 *Entry. Nestled below the loft and focused on one window of the focal array opposite the bed, an intimate subspace receives the visitor and leads him around the encountered bed beyond the low wall.*

fig. 6 *Sitting below the liberated ceiling, the triumphant loft desk serves as the attenuated headboard for the bed. The bath beckons to the left, situated at the half level between the entry and the loft. The modest and obscured entry is to the right, sitting below the aforementioned loft. Note the veiled power of the tantalizingly exposed brick to the upper right. Note also the use of skylights.*

Photos by Louis Mackall

cally increasing window pattern whose spacing grew to become a large picture window focusing on the huge maple tree just beyond the addition.

With the bed and desk in competition for the same spot in the plan, it was decided to raise the desk above the back of the bed. The centered loft space created would sit above closets (properly opaque), and the wall supporting the desk would serve as a headboard for the bed.

With the curving wall kept free, a bank of closet space was placed near the entry (which was located at the head of the stairs), leaving the bath to occupy the other side of the plan.

The bath became the pivotal space for the entire room. Traditionally, the bath is as opaque as the closet, and its relocation to the far corner of the room makes it invisible until the bed has been circumnavigated. This emboldened the architects enough to ask if the clients wouldn't mind an open bath, with the toilet and shower isolated but the sinks and Jacuzzi nestled in one corner. To the architects' delight, the clients had no reservations. Since the hot tub and desk loft needed vertical access and the bath did need some sense of its own space, it was elevated four steps up from the bedroom floor.

A cascade of levels is thus created. From the squeezed perspective of entry occurring under the low desk loft, the space fairly explodes upon entry. As the head tilts up, skylights and the ascending forms described catch the eye. The spiraling sequence of form and space finally serves to recondense the space above the original point of entry, the crowning desk loft, the cockpit for the entire addition.

Two important things are done by this sequence. First, bodies pirouette as they walk in, defusing the tendency to focus on the center of the window array. Second, the spatial whirlwind has the bed as the eye of its kinetic path. The sense of bed as placid center is reinforced, which is only natural given that the entire series of events created only serves to glorify the act of sleeping.

By creating this heavenly haven for a marriage, Louis Mackall and his partner have given the house a culminating and controlling focus. Perhaps a transition in the way we live can be seen in this project. The shift of the perceived center of the house from the formal front door to the most intimate and informal of spaces, the new bedroom, signals a departure from the rigid focus of frontality in favor of a less fixed, more spiritual outlook.

5

6

LIVING ROOMS AND FRONT DOORS

The need for functional versatility, the requirements of
connection with the great outdoors, and a
rethinking of the formal entry to a house
have helped revise the perception of
the living room and front door.

INTRODUCTION

Typically the American formal living room is a
stilted space. Often the square footage of the
home has been preemptively divided into several
distinct spaces creating an assemblage of living
room, dining room, and den that takes limited space
and creates several undersized and arbitrarily divided rooms. Such subdivisions usually create
wasteful and disruptive circulation patterns. In the
typical American home, the formal living room tends
to be individually symmetrical, showing a static,
centered approach to space.

The days of the plastic slipcover are ending.
Fewer homes have pianos no one plays, fireplaces
that go unlit, and carpets stretching wall to wall
over hardwood floors. The living room of the 1980s
must have the utility and the flexibility made impossible by the size and form of the traditional living room. A concurrent benefit of this newfound
openness can be an enhanced sense of perspective
upon entry to the house.

The need for connection with the outside world
is a natural result of the desire for open space. Over
the past thirty years, we have stopped thinking of
the functional requirements of windows and doors
(catching light and providing access) as mutually
exclusive. The living room can best utilize the spatial liberation and functional expansion a deck can
provide. Perhaps the cheapest cost-per-foot space
available, the well-designed deck can be the major
indoor-outdoor mediator in a home.

Often a concurrent development in a living room
addition or renovation is the sun space. Obviously
the siting of the existing building and the internal
layout are crucial in the viable creation of a solar-
gain space. Rather than being a tack-on, prefab, semi-
industrial greenhouse, the sun space can be merely
a glazed wall or the modern equivalent of French
doors facing a terrace or deck. Additionally, the hot
tub can often be in close proximity to the main living area, integrated with whatever inside-outside
interface exists.

Obviously the primary function of such spaces
is public accommodation during social gatherings,
but since the nature of entertaining has evolved from
sit-down eating and adjourning for sex-separated
conversation to more ongoing eating, drinking, and
talking, the location of the living room relative to
the kitchen and bath has become more direct. With
the new emphasis on electronic entertainment—
video, stereo, etc.—the number of functional requirements has multiplied.

It is not enough to provide a large open area. An
architect must use his broader perspective and
training to exploit the opportunities a living room
addition affords in solving problems beyond simple
spatial expansion. Entry, circulation, multipurpose
space planning, and spatial hierarchy should be addressed when designing the major space of the
American home. The following additions evidence
all of these challenges well met.

Outside In

By selective removal, Peter Bohlin transforms a farmhouse.

PROJECT PROFILE

Graham residence
Location: Dallas, Pa.
Architect: Peter Bohlin,
Bohlin/Powell/Larkin/Cywinski
Budget: $75,000
Area renovated: 2600 ft²
Area added: None

Soon after Sally and Tucker Graham married, they purchased a nineteenth-century farmhouse. The victim of a fire, it had been open to the elements for a year. The Grahams called in Peter Bohlin to investigate the damage and recommend those technical solutions required to arrest the rot and structurally repair and seal up the envelope of the house.

After much good work, Bohlin went over his recommendations with the Grahams for the repair of the neglected building. At the end of his report, he offhandedly remarked that the Grahams might "someday consider opening up the back." Tucker Graham's eyes lit up, much to the surprise of Peter Bohlin. It seemed that although the house was spatially adequate, years of addition and remodeling had left the core, the living room, rather dim. And since Tucker Graham sold fine furniture, the paucity of light saddened his prospect of displaying his personal collection of furnishings. The need to save an endangered building was absolutely imperative to the Grahams, but the aesthetic concerns, although latent, became the over-riding intention for the entire renovation.

The unintended result of the house's past was to create a U shape with wings extending to the north and flanking the original central stair. Revisions had created a cacophony of discordant windows and siding surfaces. The agglomerated form and random interior organization left a limp blob of architecture for all to see and be puzzled by.

No front door was evident, as it was hidden by an aluminum window-glazed sun porch, but the back door screamed for use, being nakedly exposed to the street. Inside, one room bled into the next, and doors at every corner prevented any sequence from manifesting itself. Most discouraging of all, the beautiful northerly perspective was completely unappreciable from the interior. In short, this was a farmhouse with no visible farm.

Bohlin attacked the problems by realizing the house was quite flabby—devoid of

OWNER'S STATEMENT

After purchasing a century-old farmhouse that had been substantially fire-damaged, we recognized the need of a professional to guide our thinking.

A need to open up the house to some of its beautiful surroundings was the number one priority. We desired a light and airy environment that would complement our contemporary furnishings and at the same time preserve some of the more traditional characteristics of the house.

Working with Peter Bohlin on this renovation was certainly a pleasure, and we were most pleased with the result. —*Tucker Graham*

ARCHITECT'S STATEMENT

Rather than editing out all inconsistencies, we have taken pleasure in the strange mix of trim, windows, and shutters on the house's exterior and its somewhat awkward massing. We have thought of this renovation as another step in the evolutionary life of the building, strengthening the interior's psychological connection to the garden and heightening the house's light and spatial qualities through the "simple" device of opening up the stair and its exterior wall. —*Peter Bohlin*

order or thrill while being overly ample in terms of square footage.

Rather than reject the quality of bucolic informality, Bohlin chose to reinforce it by making all siding and fenestration detailing relatively consistent. But most important, Bohlin saw the necessity for one ordering element that would make sense of the entire building. Fortunately, the unique functional quality of the central stair coincided with the crotch of the U shape in the existing house. So where a formal focal point met a functional one, Bohlin eliminated the entire facade facing north, replaced clapboards with glazing, and removed part of the floor separating the two levels. The flanking sides of the U prevented visual intrusion from the street and framed the northerly view with a quiet dignity. Additionally, the subtle north light allowed perfect illumination for the living area and provided a welcoming axis to the outside world.

Having given the house a backbone, Bohlin next solved the problem of the obscured entry. The most obvious solution would have been to create a new entry, some expressed focal point, proud and distinct. In the path of any revisionist entry addition stood the aforementioned 1920s glazed front porch, whose foundations and floor were of rather attractive stone construction. Again using the awkward existing features to his advantage, Bohlin reglazed the walls, pulling back the entry wall under the existing sun-porch roof to align with the diagonal line of the roof's existing hip. In creating a diagonal element in an orthogonal context, the architect facilitated a visual indication of entry and allowed for the type of detailing that contrasted with the existing conditions.

With both the front door and the stair solutions, Peter Bohlin allowed the opportunity for modern expression by creating a consistent traditional datum over the rest of the body of the house. By the reduction of mass in both areas, he perforated a stultifying skin—allowing the outside in and allowing the inside to become part of the world around it.

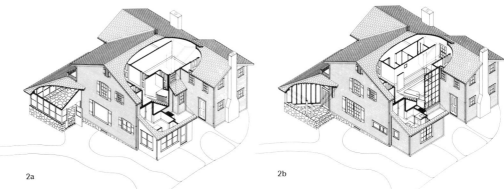

2a   2b

fig. 1 *North elevation. Framed and nurtured by the existing flanking wings, the new stair wall gives focus and hierarchy to an otherwise random massing.*

fig. 2 *Isometrics (a) before and (b) after. The existing building had multiple window and siding types. By making all windows and siding relatively harmonious, the architect allowed the new stair window to take on a fresh and singular position. Note also the inviting new entry and the lack of visual confusion over where to enter the house.*

Line drawings by the architect

Graham Residence   87

fig. 3 *Stair wall. With the eaves and clapboards aligned and the glazing stretched to reach the side walls, the new opening focuses attention within. Note the small square interior window on the second floor. It is connected to the master bedroom closet, allowing the owners to see who is at their back door (right foreground) and causing guests to inquire about the Grahams' unique fabric collage.*

fig. 4 *Existing stair wall.*

fig. 5 *Lower-level plan. The new diagonal entry wall and reglazed porch create a recognition of entry once lost.*

3

4

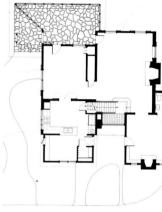

5

6

7   *Joseph W. Molitor*

fig. 6 *View from head of stair. The simplified rail opens up the stairwell space to embrace the second-floor corridor.*

fig. 7 *View from stair interior.*

fig. 8 *New entry wall.*

8   *Joseph W. Molitor*

A Lovely Lantern

*Donlyn Lyndon reaches above the tyranny
of single-story suburbia.*

With 2000 books crowding their living room and no room in their home for guests to spend the night, Shelia and David Littlejohn cried out for help to Donlyn Lyndon of Lyndon/Buchanan Associates.

Lyndon knew that the existing living room area was spatially inadequate, but he also recognized the general flaws of the modest single-story structure tucked in a tight lot in Kensington, California. The unrelentingly low eave height of the existing house was at best unassuming and at worst deadly dull. The building confronted visitors with a similarly prosaic garage thrust forward on the front lawn, obscuring the front door entry to the house. Lastly, there was a paucity of light in the living area due to the shading of the garage and the position of the living room at the far corner of the home's U-shaped configuration, effectively preventing all afternoon light from penetrating the space.

In a simple and bold stroke, Lyndon addressed these several sticky problems with a solution that seems effortless. By extending the living room to the south, Lyndon realized the intrinsic intention of the original building plan to form an entry courtyard. Having manifested literally what was once only implied, the architect broke the oppressive horizontal roof line with a simple two-story tower with clerestory windows facing south.

This civilized vertical statement solved a multitude of problems. Besides creating an

OWNER'S STATEMENT

Our sensible, ordinary California house was becoming very cramped, with 2000 books stored in the master bedroom, a study in one corner of the living room, and no place for overnight guests. We decided to build this addition after we realized that either moving to a larger house or building on a second floor—two earlier dreams—had been driven out of our reach by inflation.

The architect devoted a very generous amount of time and thought to this small but perfect addition. He kept finding ways to add space, light, and amenities—and to hold down our costs at the same time.

The building process was a joyful time, in which our whole family shared, partly because the scheme allowed us to observe it all from an essentially undisturbed original house, partly because the builder and his crew turned out to be such amiable, skilled, and thoughtful people.

Donlyn's tower and Shelia's court (it was my wife's idea) have made our whole house very special. We are delighted with the way this imaginative addition has freed and enhanced the *rest* of the house, giving us a set of rooms that seems spacious and altogether new.

If we *could* have moved to a larger house, I'm convinced we couldn't have done any better. —*David Littlejohn*

event for the meek massing of the original house to play off of, the tower signaled entry. By "waving" to those who encounter the building, the tower nullifies the garage's obscuring effect. To reinforce this intention, Lyndon provided an arbor to link garage and house at the entry to the newly created courtyard, thus indicating entry at eye level.

In the best tradition of Britain's Ely Cathedral, Lyndon's tower serves as a modest "lantern" trapping south light and taking it into the addition. Besides giving the benefits of a light well's diffused luminescence, the tower serves as a flue, allowing its heated air to draw the stagnant summer atmosphere out of the house.

With so much ambient light coming down from the tower, Lyndon could afford to cover the single-story walls of the addition with adequate bookshelves for the Littlejohns' impressive book collection.

Lyndon's tower could easily have been detailed in a manner insulting the existing meek house. Lyndon allowed the stucco skirt that serves as the house's exterior wainscot to become the exterior skin of the tower. In doing so, he expressed a difference without creating a disdainful dissonance with the existing building.

This project is quite remarkable for its calculated drama born of a meager budget. In solving so many problems for so little money, Lyndon has evidenced the fruits of an innovative heart and a clear head.

ARCHITECTS' STATEMENT

The project uses the addition to form a courtyard and make a new entry to the house. The library is built very simply with high south windows above the bookshelves, a tile floor, and a light tower that captures midday sun in a place that can also have through ventilation when needed. A tight budget was also a concern.

—*Lyndon/Buchanan Associates*

fig. 1 *Tower interior.*

fig. 2 *Exterior view. By its verticality, the applied tower "waves" hello to the prospective entrant.*

fig. 3 *View into tower. Light cascades from south-facing windows. Note column to left.*

1

2

3

5

fig. 4 *Tower entrance. Bold overhang and French doors provide an embracing low-scale indication of entry on a vertical facade.*

fig. 5 *Exit axis. Framing the view, the encountered elements allow for a sense of planned travel.*

fig. 6 *Plan. Addition shown by solid black lines of plan. Note courtyard formed by the addition and the entry sequence of threshold and trellis near top of plan. Tower can be seen as little nub at top of added space.*

fig. 7 *Addition interior. Clerestory windows allow for massive bookcases with no loss of light level. Note chaise longue guest bed in foreground. Note also tower support support column to right.*

Line drawing by the architect
Photos by Lyndon/Buchanan Associates

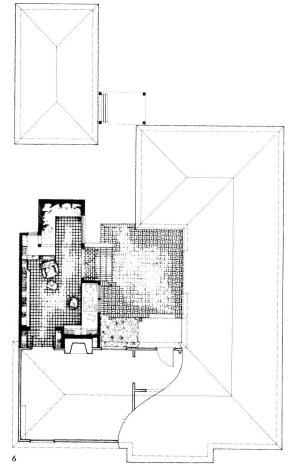

6

4

7

Divide and Conquer

An informal recreation room becomes the focus of a house and its site.

PROJECT PROFILE

Lohman residence
Location: McLean, Va.
Architects: Cass & Pinnell
Budget: Not available
Area renovated: None
(in this phase)
Area added: 350 ft²

Lila Scott Lohman and her new husband, Mark Lohman, had just combined families. In truth, there was an overabundance of teenagers and just not enough space in one house, but love will out. There was no basement to be paneled, the garage was already slated for second-story bedrooms, and the attic was full of the stuff that should have been in the basement. Rather than run a youth hostel, it appeared far more productive to create a home with a simple spatial expansion.

What to do? When the sink backs up, you call a plumber, and Lila Scott Lohman called her local space decloggers, Cass & Pinnell of Washington, D.C.

It is seldom that a seemingly complex need has such a simple answer. The architects realized not only that the house had to expand but that the site had to be brought into play as an absorber of the human overflow a house full of teenagers can easily create.

In extending the new space into the backyard, on axis with the kitchen, the architects made the interior adolescent mecca easily accessible. This rudimentary planning decision had numerous ramifications. First, the tradition of this 1950s home of expanding laterally—evidenced by several addenda—was ended. Second, the backyard became divided in three parts.

Obviously the form of this added space would be seen from all sides, and it would often be used as simply a refuge from rain or sun—hence formal in form and friendly in function. This all represented a complete transformation from the original home, where the informal house rather starkly met the outside world.

OWNER'S STATEMENT

Three years ago I made a difficult decision to separate from my husband. All four of my children were teenagers, and I began to think about how I would change my home to accommodate and cope with their needs. Since my home lacked a basement, I thought perhaps a large informal family room would be ideal as a place where teenagers could bring their friends. Shortly after the task of developing the design began, I met and subsequently married a man who forever took away my idea of retiring to my own little corner.

When it became obvious that our families would merge, we had a wonderful time planning the addition together, and my house became our house and a home for us all. The entire addition has turned a nice but rather ordinary house into a really special home. —*Lila Scott Lohman*

ARCHITECTS' STATEMENT

This sprawling 1950s developer house, tucked back into the hillside of a wooded site in suburban Virginia, required several stages of modification to open up the building to views and use the backyard.

As part of our work, we responded to a request for an elegant but informal family room connected to the terraces, pool, and backyard. The large, almost freestanding room that we added connects to the den and separates the formal part of the yard and house from the less formal areas. We think that the large, simple form of the new room feels like it is the original structure to which the more random collection of rooms of the 1950s house has been added in stages. The new room has 10-foot triple-hung windows, enabling it to become an open pavilion on appropriate occasions. —*Cass & Pinnell*

To offset the mass of the existing house and respond to the multiple exposure, Cass and Pinnell gave their addition two symmetrical end gables and a lightly vertical massing that housed a quietly elegant volume of space. Every window is custom-made. Huge triple-hung glazing panels can open up to create a completely open space, while fixed clerestory eyebrow windows provide a lightly eccentric image.

By its central location and orientation, the addition was automatically the single most prominent part of the house, but by employing marginally eccentric detailing, Cass and Pinnell created a type of instant antiquity—a building whose history is storied by implication only. By enhancing its power posture with so many customized quirks, the architects turned all eyes away from the rather dull existing house.

The idea that a single piece can transform an entire building is not unprecedented, but this structure goes quite far in rendering its parent building (over four times its size) relatively unimportant to the casual observer.

These ambiguities of age, image, and use all converge to give the building a layer of mystery that can only be felt not analyzed. The addition uses the existing building's siding and roof material, but the other elements of the construction—form, structure, windows and doors, detailing, and space defined—are unprecedented. More than unprecedented, the new form is a more than subtle rejection of the existing building's mediocrity and catalog convenient detailing. In this addition, Cass and Pinnell reverse the rules of the existing house and transform the entire site.

fig. 1 *Inside view, looking toward formal gardens. Lighting serves to enhance the theatrical quality of the windows. Note the stark tie-rod ensemble above.*

fig. 2 *Formal facade. A haunting form, the eyebrow windows serve to enhance the monolithic nature of the upper facade, while the oversized lower openings create several false scale indications.*

fig. 3 *Formal garden vista. The new addition utilizes tne existing building's materials, and its openings are also unprecedented and yet related to the original house. This court uses an arbor pavilion and low walls to focus interest and define space.*

Photos by the architects

1

2

3

Custom Look, Prefab Price

Zar & Hicks do a lot with a little.

PROJECT PROFILE

Blum residence
Location: Chicago, Ill.
Architects: Zar & Hicks
Budget: $7100
Area renovated: 200 ft^2
Area added: None

The commom public perception is that the noun "architect" has a direct relationship to the adjective "expensive." Given the nature of the design projects that receive the most journalistic recognition, this association would be a reasonable assumption for the average homeowner. In this particular project, however, creativity was not blind to some very tight purse strings, and the limited budget fostered a great deal of ingenuity.

As a corollary to the word-association game above, Katsuko and Fred Blum of Chicago always associated the word "custom" with two words: "beautiful" as well as, to their frustration, the familiar "expensive."

Undaunted by their fears, the couple brought a very specific problem to the architecture office of Angela Maria Zar and Bill Hicks. The spiritual focus of the Blums' backyard, and perhaps the entire house, was a nearby church steeple. Unfortunately the only way to gaze at its graceful form from within the house was to stand at the back door.

The Blums' urban house had a typically narrow rear elevation containing the aforementioned back door and a small deck, naked to the world. Behind this inhospitable deck was a screen porch set too deeply into the house for an uninterrupted view of the steeple. Both spaces were too small to entertain in.

Obviously the spaces had to be combined. Obviously some new enclosure was needed to cover the front porch. But most obvious of all to the Blums was that their small budget seemingly preempted anything but a clumsy stock solution that would ruin their view of the steeple.

Keeping the limits of scope and money in mind, the Zar and Hicks design duet cautiously suggested that through careful contracting and salvaging of the in-place foundation, both the Blums' view and budget could be accommodated. If the Blums were willing to shop for inexpensive materials

OWNERS' STATEMENT

This wonderful porch combined a preexisting narrow open deck, rarely used, with a small screened porch, too small for entertaining. It was made into a larger lovely area where we spend much of the time during the warm season relaxing, dining, and entertaining.

An important consideration in extending the porch was to have a glass roof so as not to obstruct the light and the picturesque view of the church steeple visible during foliage-free seasons. The architects' inventive design, rendered to fit our limited budget, produces a dramatic effect with curved forms integrating the greenhouse section, yet the contemporary style fits well into our late-nineteenth-century house.

—*The Blums*

ARCHITECTS' STATEMENT

This commission had the following criteria:

1. If possible, use the existing deck framing for the expansion of the enclosed porch.

2. Create a design to meet a very tight budget.

3. Create an environment that would enhance the view to a distant steeple.

The solutions to the problems were as follows:

1. A stock component greenhouse glazing system was used.

2. The shape of the greenhouse element was repeated in three wood bents (two adjacent to the greenhouse and one freestanding).

3. To execute the work, the owner employed a contractor who employs artists moonlighting as carpenters. With this type of work force, the porch was constructed as though it were a piece of sculpture.

—*Zar & Hicks*

and research their options, money could be saved.

Perhaps the least expensive permanent watertight enclosure is the prefabricated greenhouse. Made of mass-produced, interchangeable parts, every component combines both structure and finish surface. The Blums were afraid that a greenhouse facing west would be a bit silly and that framing their steeple with such an industrialized glazing system would taint the vista for them. Zar and Hicks, on the other hand, understood that the standard greenhouse represents a system of parts, and some of those parts were perfectly suited for this application.

Ideally, the new enclosure should frame and focus the view and simultaneously allow an unlimited vertical appreciation of the spire. By utilizing only the glazing panels of a standard greenhouse and making the end pieces bold sculptural elements, the architects could make the industrial quality of the glazing system relatively unnoticeable.

A hybrid construction of existing deck, custom wood bents, expressed lighting, and greenhouse glazing was created. The exterior form has a poetic high-tech sensibility, being an informally Constructivist combination of standard domestic finish carpentry interfacing with stainless steel and aluminum pieces. Making the construction detailing disintegral and allowing some pieces to stand proud or bypass other pieces heightens the effect and lowers the construction costs.

It should be noted, however, that this is an unheated though finished space. Without the need for airtight insulated construction, detailing can be fairly loose fit, as can be seen in this project.

But as with all successful addition projects, the end did indeed justify and enrich the means. The Blums can sit with their friends, sheltered, focused, and continually delighted with the unique forms and innovative detailing.

fig. 1 *Exterior. This romantically softened High Tech construction creates a new back door and unheated but protected informal living space. Note the purely ornamental wood bent at left and the use of stainless steel as an ornamental finish surface. Note also that the column supports were retained from the original deck.*

Photos by Fred Leavitt

1

3

4

fig. 2 *End view. Heavy door frame and heavier wood bent bypass each other.*

fig. 3 *Inside. Obscured by summer growth, the steeple view focused upon by the addition is best appreciated in leafless seasons. Note the interior use of the stainless steel on the underside of the wood bents. Note that the side walls are screens not glazing.*

fig. 4 *Exterior view.*

Suburban Sophisticate

*The firm of Leung Hemmler Camayd transforms
a typical builder's bi-level house
into a beautiful home.*

PROJECT PROFILE

Sheer residence
Location: Grouse Hill, Pa.
Architects: Leung Hemmler
Camayd
Budget: $135,000 (includes all
work done)
Area renovated: 1300 ft^2
Area added: 2144 ft^2

OWNERS' STATEMENT

Our project is the result of considerable thought and discussion. We liked many things about our original house, but it had several shortcomings. We felt we needed additional space. While our house was quite comfortable for our family of three, when guests came to share a week or weekend, we felt cramped.

Our second space requirement was for an adequate study. With two professional people in the household, we had a need for room to accommodate an unusual number of books and journals.

The house is located in a naturalistic setting with a spectacular view that would be difficult to duplicate.

Renovating the existing structure and adding a new section accomplished our goals and transformed an ordinary house into a unique home.
—*The Sheers*

ARCHITECTS' STATEMENT

The young family of three liked their location and the swimming pool. They desired more entertaining space and a more luxurious master bedroom. Given the amount of space that was to be added, we investigated the possibility of starting from scratch. We found that comparable lots in the neighborhood were no longer available. Also, our clients were concerned about having a place to live during the construction period.

Adding on was the realistic way to achieve the dual goals of having a more gracious home and staying in the same neighborhood. We decided to wrap the addition around the pool and to completely change the point of entry. That allowed us to take advantage of the views, to shelter the pool area, and to give the house a face parallel to the road.
—*Leung Hemmler Camayd*

As with many homes in recent affluent suburban developments, the actual building owned by George and Barbara Sheer was far less impressive than the location, view, and ancillary amenities. The Sheers also needed more room to grow and provide for two professionals under one roof.

But the young family of three had the realization that it was not simply a matter of inadequate space that had to be addressed. The Sheers knew that their personality as a family just did not mesh with the thoroughly uninspiring aesthetics of their bourgeois bi-level. Obviously not so much designed as just plain built, their home had a rectilinear regularity that rendered it spiritually inert.

The Sheers made the decision that in order to maintain ownership of their pool, their view, and their sanity, they had to remake their residence in a different image. That decision created the need for an architect, and the firm of Leung Hemmler Camayd was ready, willing, and able to take on the project.

As with most simply framed houses, the lack of differentiated massing prevented any external indications of entry, function, or site orientation. Too little of the house faced views. The backyard pool stood naked for the world to see. There was no recognition of the sun's available heat and light. In short, in building a structure to generate a healthy profit, the developer of this subdivision had rejected any deviation from a standardized design.

The architects set about to infuse the existing building with a vital responsiveness left out of the original design. Given the need to add about as much space as was already present in the house, they decided to transform the simplistic oblong form into a variated composition of connected shapes, refuting the aesthetically parched image that accompanies profitability.

Whereas all functions originally were combined in a single subdivided box, Leung Hemmler Camayd decided to create a distinctly separate entry and a similarly expressive living room. They oriented these new parts to transform the plain rectangle of the existing floor plan into an L shape wrapping around the existing pool.

In reorienting the entry, the architects realized a secondary benefit. Since the entry now lay at the intersection of the two legs of the L and bypassed the original structure, the existing living room could become a grand master bedroom complete with fireplace.

Concurrently, a remodeled kitchen and new master bath displaced the existing dining room into the new addition. The architects placed the new dining area on axis with the entrance but separated it by a change in level, thus creating an inviting spatial embrace upon entry.

The new living room addition was designed as two spaces using minor level changes. The main living area is adjacent to the entry and dining space and is centered on a new fireplace. The secondary living space took the form of a south-facing solarium set three steps above the main living room. Interior windows connect the spaces and form an ascending circulation sequence that wraps around the existing pool.

Since the entire house was addressed in terms of planning, reworking of the entire exterior was in order. The existing plywood siding was replaced with vertical cedar siding. Eaves were broadened and a trellised porch was added off the newly converted master bedroom.

All of these softening touches helped diffuse the brutishly arbitrary nature of an average American suburban home. It is a sad commentary on the state of middle-income residential building design when a relatively new home needs so much work to undo the thoughtlessness of the original building.

There is a special joy in righting a wrong, even if it is born of nothing more malicious than profit-hungry expediency. The careful consideration by Leung Hemmler Camayd shows a willingness to address existing situations and make the best of them. Would that the average suburban home design was created with such sensibilities.

2

fig. 1 *Entry. This is the lone vertical element in the formal massing of the house; great red doors and outsized clerestory window beckon the prospective entrant. Flanking infill glazing and aligned eaves broken by the entry tower help reinforce the assertive quality of this element.*

fig. 2 *Entry interior. As seen from the raised dining room, the entry space allows for even, natural lighting and an openness not possible in a traditionally delineated space. Note that the built-in sideboard is centered on the entry and serves as a visual barrier for those entering the house. (The highly polished tabletop reflects the flanking window, creating the illusion of a void under the sideboard.)*

Photos and line drawing by the architects

1

Sheer Residence   101

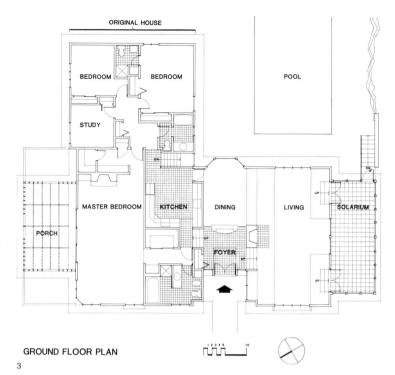

ORIGINAL HOUSE

fig. 3 *Ground-floor plan. The new porch (with new garage underneath) and the wing for the entry, dining and living areas, and solarium flank the existing building. Note the recessed entry and corresponding bay window opposite. Note also how the addition creates a courtyard for the pool.*

fig. 4 *Front elevation. A diffused, relaxed facade, the bedroom-end gable (left) and living-room-end gable (right) frame the new entry tower form. Those gable elements are in turn bracketed by the sun space (right) and the master bedroom deck-trellis (left). Note that the entry was completely reoriented to the west elevation from the north side of the building.*

GROUND FLOOR PLAN

3

5

6 7

fig. 5 Living room. Symmetrical arrangement of elements creates a placid sense of order. Interior windows looking into the solarium and a mirrored cabinet back reflecting the windows opposite create a subtle ambiguity of inside versus outside. Note that the clerestory windows are operable, allowing for good ventilation in summer and convection of solar-heated air in winter.

fig. 6 Solarium interior. Simple framing and an avoidance of custom components help make this an affordable amenity. The wood interior surfaces and exterior lighting fixtures help create the sense of exterior architecture brought inside. The fan helps vent solar-heated air in summer and keep solar-heated air at the level of occupancy during winter.

fig. 7 Master bedroom deck. Not relating to the living room addition but added on the roof of a new garage to the north, this exterior room is the skeletal counterpart to the solarium on the opposite side of the house. Note the repetition of the muntin pattern of the entry clerestory window.

Far-reaching Renovation

*Changing needs make a carriage
house into a home.*

The owner of an estate in Waverly, Pennsylvania, had two problems; how to sell a property that was too big for prospective buyers and where to go once the estate had been sold.

With one bold stroke, both problems were solved. By renovating an existing carriage house on her estate, the owner could provide a home for herself and a way to make her property a salable commodity. Good ideas often have discouraging results, but in the case of this particular notion, an extraordinary home evolved from a glorified garage.

The firm of Leung Hemmler Camayd was called in to transform prosaic space into a house for sophisticated country living. The most obvious missing element was a human-scaled entry. When the carriage house was built, most openings to it were scaled for a horse, an auto, or maintenance equipment, and those entrances for people provided convenient access and little else.

The owner wished to maintain a light touch on the visual impact of this publicly situated building, yet a means of creating privacy from the street was desperately needed. Where once the building itself served as a barrier from the outside world for the estate, now the carriage house cum retirement residence needed a screen for its front yard.

So the architects took the need for said barrier, combined it with the need for a formal entry, and, using an extension of the existing building's architectural vernacular, created a marvelous event. A wing wall was built, springing from an existing alcove and given a lightly bowed arc to animate the indication of entry.

The wall was surfaced in the same stucco as the existing house, and had its height determined by the height of the existing alcove detailing. To add some visual zest, the

PROJECT PROFILE

Carriage House
Location: Waverly, Pa.
Architects: Leung Hemmler Camayd
Budget: $125,000 (includes entire restoration)
Area renovated: 4000 ft²
Area added: 400 ft²

OWNER'S STATEMENT

The time had come to sell the large and lovely family homestead where I had spent the greater part of my life.

No prospective buyer seemed interested in all the acreage and delightful perquisites of a real country home—greenhouse, stable, cold frames, "rabbit" house (which had once housed all sorts of appropriate animals and birds)—literally the playground of my childhood and that of my children.

The large, 40 × 60 feet, carriage house or stable seemed to provide four wonderfully solid walls in which to develop a new but somehow comfortably old and easy-to-care-for house—one that now really feels like home.

ARCHITECTS' STATEMENT

This carriage house-stable, located at the most public corner of a country estate, was often eyed by its owner as a potential restoration project.

The strongest impression we received from the client was the desire for informality. We achieved this through the creation of a series of open, horizontal spaces and avoidance of the Classical details that we love. The most used areas, the living-dining room, the kitchen-greenhouse, and the den, are contained by the sweeping curve. The intent here is to relate all spaces to the terrace, deck, and garden beyond. Entry to the house is from a somewhat private lane. The curved form outside screens the terrace from the lane and carries one to the door tucked within the existing building.

—*Leung Hemmler Camayd*

architects capped their entry wall with an arbor, creating a far-reaching transition sequence leading into the house.

With the wall shielding the front yard from view and the arbor reaching out to welcome the potential visitor, the interior had much promise to fulfill. The existing stables were removed, and all the amenities of a modern home were installed within the interior. In their planning, the architects found one element missing: natural light.

A carriage house is designed to be deep enough to accommodate two rows of stables with a space between for access. Hence it is deeper than most average homes. Given this depth of space for light to penetrate and the paucity of windows present in a carriage house, a second exterior gesture was called for: a greenhouse.

Fortunately the building faced south. Even more fortunately, there existed a porch that could easily provide the shell for a greenhouse addition. The light brought in by the new glazing provided a rich reward for those having experienced the thoughtful entry sequence described.

It would have been easy to remove the stable influence (so to speak) completely from the structure and create an urbane flat inside an affluently rustic shell. But the owner opted to refit many of the existing components of the barn in new applications, creating an elegant informality of civilized relaxation. Barn doors are reused as room partitions, interior beaded tongue-and-groove paneling is reused, and the existing columns and beams are not removed (although sheathed in new finish materials).

The large expanse of living space harboring the kitchen is open and yet scaled for human use by the furniture and elements sitting in it. The architects applied an arcing interior wall on the north side of

1

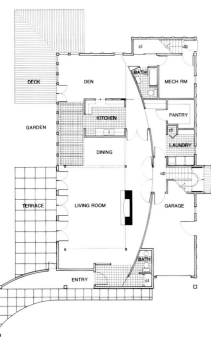

2

fig. 1 *Entry wall and arbor. The effect of extending existing lines and planes is seen in this fluid delineator. The existing alcove floor extends to become the pediment for the wall, as the horizontal banding becomes a three-dimensional datum for the curving stucco wall, which in turn is animated from the alcove side wall. Providing separation from the street, this element also offers an invitation to enter with a elongated sequence of progressively enclosed spaces. The busy rhythm of shadow lines offers yet another beckoning feature in this controlled kinetic ensemble.*

fig. 2 *First-floor plan. The newly imposed curves on the entry and on the north side of the living room form the architects' signature for the new work done. Note the enclosed porch cum greenhouse opposite the kitchen and the terrace, deck, and entry extensions from the original building.*

Photos by Otto Baitz

fig. 3 *The newly enclosed greenhouse maintains the horizontal banding that existed in the original building. The low deck provides well-defined exterior space, while the patio adjacent to the new entry wall (right) serves as a less defined social-overflow accommodation. Note the reused stable door situated in the new exterior entry wall.*

fig. 4 *Entry elevation. An existing entry alcove at the corner of the carriage house extends to become an indication of entry and a visual screen shielding the front yard from public view. Note how the first-floor cornice banding extends to become a datum upon which the arbor rests.*

fig. 5 *Greenhouse: A sloped ceiling follows the existing roof pitch, into which skylights are set. A simple opening (right) indicates the presence of the kitchen, which is conveniently located as the greenhouse also serves as the informal dining area. Note the use of barn doors at the rear of the space. Note, too, the quarry-tile floor for heat gain, complete with a drain for ease of cleanup.*

fig. 6 *Entry vista. Once through a small air lock, the visitor is welcomed by an expanse of open space where a variety of surface finishes, furnishings, and light levels create a happy variety of events, culminating in the greenhouse in the left center. Note the reuse of the barn doors as room dividers, remounted on the original tracks.*

4

3

5

6

the room to focus attention to the glazed south wall facing the newly defined front yard.

To further civilize the site, a deck and patio were extended into the yard and relate respectively to a den and living room.

By creating a light eccentricity in the elements applied to the existing building, the architects evidenced a contemporary touch without distorting the original quality of the house. The architects have not only provided a new use for an old structure, they have lent new meaning to the architecture they encountered and have helped create renewed delight in a familiar context.

All Decked Out

*Jersey Devil creates a fabulous adult playpen
in Locust Grove, Virginia.*

It was bad enough that the deck around Ed and Trudy Lefrak's vacation house was too small and had no view. When it became obvious to the couple that most of the supporting pole structure was rotten and in danger of collapse, you would have been hard-pressed to tell them that it was all for the best.

The Lefraks located Jersey Devil, an itinerant band of designers who more often than not build their designs. It was soon diagnosed that the deck and pole structural decay was beginning to impact badly on the house. It was indeed time to act.

With the energy and conviction of skilled hands and applied minds, the Jersey Devil crew wasted no time in removing the rampant rot, repairing and reworking the existing foundation system, and simultaneously designing a new deck for the Lefraks.

An aside on exterior wood: Two fundamental problems helped cause the rapid deterioration of the pole structure and deck. First, the wood was untreated and proved to be very tasty to hungry bacteria. Second, the sheltered location helped keep the sun from drying out the wood for long periods of time, greatly enhancing the bacterial appetite. It never makes sense to use untreated wood in damp exterior conditions.

The original cramped and repressed deck having frustrated the Lefraks for years, they were more than eager to unleash the full creative energies of Jersey Devil. Besides serving the usual functions of accommodating a view or a social gathering, this deck served as the main entry to the house. The Lefraks also wanted to escape from under the excessive overhangs of the existing house. Lastly, it was determined that this deck would aggressively seek an unobstructed view of nearby Lake of the Woods.

What resulted is perhaps the most ambitious deck possible for a house of this size.

PROJECT PROFILE

Lefrak residence
Location: Locust Grove, Va.
Architect: Steve Badanes,
Jersey Devil
Budget: $14,000
Area renovated: 500 ft^2 (deck)
Area added: 500 ft^2 (deck)

OWNERS' STATEMENT

When we're here, we spend most of our time outside, so carefully planned exterior space was a high priority. Separate dining areas for children and adults have really worked out, and the tower was an unexpected bonus. The deck-tower complex replaced a rotting deck that was basically little more than a 6-foot skirt around the house and was unusable for all practical purposes.

—Ed and Trudy Lefrak

ARCHITECT'S STATEMENT

After repairing and replacing what structure we had to, we replaced the existing deck and added the new decks and tower. The "wave" forms were suggested by the lakeside site, hence curved rail sections and three "breakers" of seating (which provide privacy from neighbors) were created. The tower was located by standing on the deck and spotting the area of the tree canopy that would afford the best views.

By girdling the house with decks, we changed the image of the house from Grumpy Tyrolean to Lakeside Moderne, complete with miles of poor man's ship railing (1½-inch fir closet-pole stock). —Steve Badanes

The nearby lake had a latent design-generative effect during the days of rot removal and structural renewal. Somehow the image of the lake kept appearing in the back of resident Devil Steve Badanes's mind.

It became apparent that this deck would draw heavily on the nature of waves and water for its forms. The cascading forms of breakers hitting the beach became three integral seats. Where it made sense to have an object—seat, table, rail, etc.—built into the deck itself, the deck surface was made to lap up to the object, bending its flat plane with a liquidity not often found in deck design.

The most prominent element of the design is the tower specifically created to catch the view the Lefraks never quite got from their old deck. Standing among the trees, the form, joinery, and cross bracing combine to make an unforgettable image.

The greatly increased deck space is a revelation once the entry stair is ascended. The original deck was a simple 6-foot band wrapped around the house. Badanes has extended the deck to the point where its square footage creates the scale of a house versus the more controlled, less open sense of a room. The broad, civilized space created by the deck seems to draw the house out of its shell of massive overhangs and limited awareness of the outside world.

But the biggest single contrast with the existing house can be seen in the unrepressed kinetic quality of the deck's plan, construction, and detailing—made all the more impressive when juxtaposed with such a repressed house form. The new deck has become the living room, with the house serving to provide protected sleeping accommodations and a bathroom or two.

Surely the career combination of designing and building helps make so many complex moves seem so easy. With the added tower, increased space, and thoroughly in-

fig. 1 *The new deck. The new "wave" wall to the left extends to bypass the existing tree. Note the heroic posture of the tower.*

fig. 2 *Existing conditions. Note the semi-Swiss detailing and the sagging corner to the right.*

Photos by Steve Badanes

fig. 3 *The big picture. The "breaker" seating progresses into the foliage (note that backs double as screening devices for privacy from a nearby neighbor). The tower serves as an altar to the view.*

fig. 4 *The tower. With all sides of the tower open for close inspection, the thought and skill of the joinery is quite evident.*

fig. 5 *The tower at entry. Existing overhang is at left. Images of sleigh, gondola, carriage, crow's nest, and railroad car all fall short.*

3

4

5

tegrated furniture elements, the deck begins to become a separate and distinct environment from both the house and the outdoor world.

It is an interesting contrast that such a simple space and function should have so much care and attention lavished upon every detail. The thoroughly considered construction and detailing visible from so many levels present a very powerful image of man acting in concert with his materials and his imagination. The pictures speak for themselves.

fig. 6 *Existing overhang. Integration is ubiquitous. The tree seems as built-in as the table and benches, and the new "wave" front blends with the existing deck-rail location.*

fig. 7 *Built-in seating. Adult dining to the right, child dining to the left. Note the curving vertical support extended from the deck. Note also the simple 1½-inch standard closet-pole stock used as railing between the "breaker" seats.*

6

7

Double-Decked

A hillside home in Los Angeles spawns some dynamic decking.

PROJECT PROFILE

Simons Residence
Location: Silverlake district, Los Angeles, Calif.
Architects: Jim Adamson and Steve Badanes, Jersey Devil
Budget: $25,000
Area renovated: 200 ft^2
Area added: 60 ft^2 (interior)
750 ft^2 (deck)

OWNER'S STATEMENT

As a result of being on a hill, our house had a wonderful view and a great deal of privacy. However, it had only a small amount of usable space in the backyard, and there was limited access to it.

Initial discussions with Jersey Devil's Jim Adamson involved building on a deck to increase the usable space. Needless to say, the finished product was better than anything we had envisioned at the outset. It has totally changed the character of the house, and currently we spend more time on the deck than inside.

—*Richard Simons*

ARCHITECT'S STATEMENT

The enclosed addition replaces a small greenhouse and employs the greenhouse glazing system. The top level above the addition provides a sun deck off the bedroom, shade for the sun room, and a visually heavy top to the glass box structure of the addition.

The new deck is typically decadent, being situated above the tinsel glow of Hollywood. —*Steve Badanes*

Many suburban Los Angeles homes have remarkably similar situations. The terrific views, tight siting, and tiny backyards are all due to the steep slopes of the existing terrain.

Richard and Pam Simons own such a precariously perched home. Built in the 1950s Modernist idiom of broad glazing panels and flush stucco banding, the house had had its purity violated by a solitary greenhouse added to create an informal dining area.

The house had a modest terrace and a backyard rendered useless by the 55° slope the building sat on. Given these conditions, it is not a revolutionary idea to build a deck. It is however a smart move to find someone who knows a bit more than good toenailing technique to design and build it for you.

Fortunately, the Simons family had heard of Jersey Devil, an affiliation of artisans and architects practicing the design-build method of construction. They generally build what they design and design what they can build. Jim Adamson and Steve Badanes came out of this talent pool and offered their suggestions.

They saw that the house needed to open up and mesh with the deck, both inside in terms of orientation and outside in terms of massing and detailing. The exterior of the house was a flat skin differentiated only by the material employed. The massing was similarly inexpressive. Adamson and Badanes knew their deck would be of a Jersey Devil sensibility—a more organic construction. Without some gestures toward integration, the deck would be an overtly tacked-on construction, with the resulting house becoming a schizophrenic disaster of two forms in aesthetic collision.

The Simons saw the sense in not simply erecting the equivalent of redwood scaffolding next to their dated house and agreed to reconsider their home in light of the new deck's impact.

Adamson and Badanes started where the original greenhouse addition left off. The glazing was extended to include the dining room, thus turning the interior of the back of the house into a lens through which the deck and its vista could be viewed.

Secondly the stucco infill of the original house provided the perfect transition material at the point where deck meets house. Because of its plasticity, stucco can be the dead-flat grainless infill desirable in the Modernist box or it can be used to create the curvilinear animated form at home with a Jersey Devil design. By extending the second-story banding as a curving mass suspended above the new greenhouse, the architects allowed the horizontal plane and curvilinear geometries of the deck to be comfortably received by the existing house. A secondary deck was created behind the new stucco form, offering the existing master bedroom a fantastic perspective. Having honored the horizontal banding of the house in their addition, the designers went one step further and integrated the same stucco banding into the new deck design. The deck rail, normally of redwood construction, became a freestanding ribbon of stucco.

Having adequately blurred the distinction between the existing house and new deck, Adamson and Badanes could focus on the deck's layout and detailing. The pictures here convey far better than words the myriad intricate interactions of the elements employed. Suffice to say the normal California amenities of hot tub, built-in seating, and multilevel organization are treated with a fresh exuberance seldom seen in the now-standard deck design. A large cantilever reaches farther out than one might expect, and the various elements interact in a playful, well-crafted manner.

Bee Mittermiller

1

Richard Simons

2

Jim Adamson

3

fig. 1 *Deck upon entry. With new greenhouse to the right and new hot tub to the left creating a threshold condition, the deck's multiple geometries beckon.*

fig. 2 *The existing home.*

fig. 3 *The new deck. Note the angled and curved massing that seems to grow out from under the eave overhang. Note also the extraordinary cantilever employed.*

Simons Residence 113

fig. 4 *Greenhouse. This new single-story addition becomes the exterior transitional massing to incorporate the new deck form into the house mass. From the interior, the expanse of glazing serves to allow the decks space and vista to be fully appreciated.*

fig. 5 *View looking back to the existing house, showing animated stucco band to left, antenna sculpture in left foreground, and hot tub in center.*

fig. 6 *Deck exterior. Rakish angles and billowing curves made solid by the use of stucco. An antenna (center) sprouts lights, ribbons, bells, plants, and some vertical whimsy amid the horizontal layering. The master bedroom deck is at the left. Note the prefabricated flue-pipe segments set into the deck wall.*

fig. 7 *The big picture. As seen from the bedroom sun deck, the major focus of the new space is apparent. Functions evolve, with the monomaterial redwood construction providing the basis for so much activity. Note the flue-pipe coffee table.*

4   5

6

The construction drawings for this project verge on the diagrammatic. Obviously, in building their own designs, the architects of Jersey Devil can solve detail questions in situ and at full scale, leaving little to chance.

The stunning results of this creative reinterpretation of a contemporary cliché are due in great part to Jersey Devil's hands-on knowledge of design and building.

It would have been all too easy to gaze into the grand vista beyond the deck and let its drama be the sole focus of the design. But Jersey Devil had the good sense and creative insight to turn around and see how the house looked from the deck's perspective. For that the Simons family is eternally grateful.

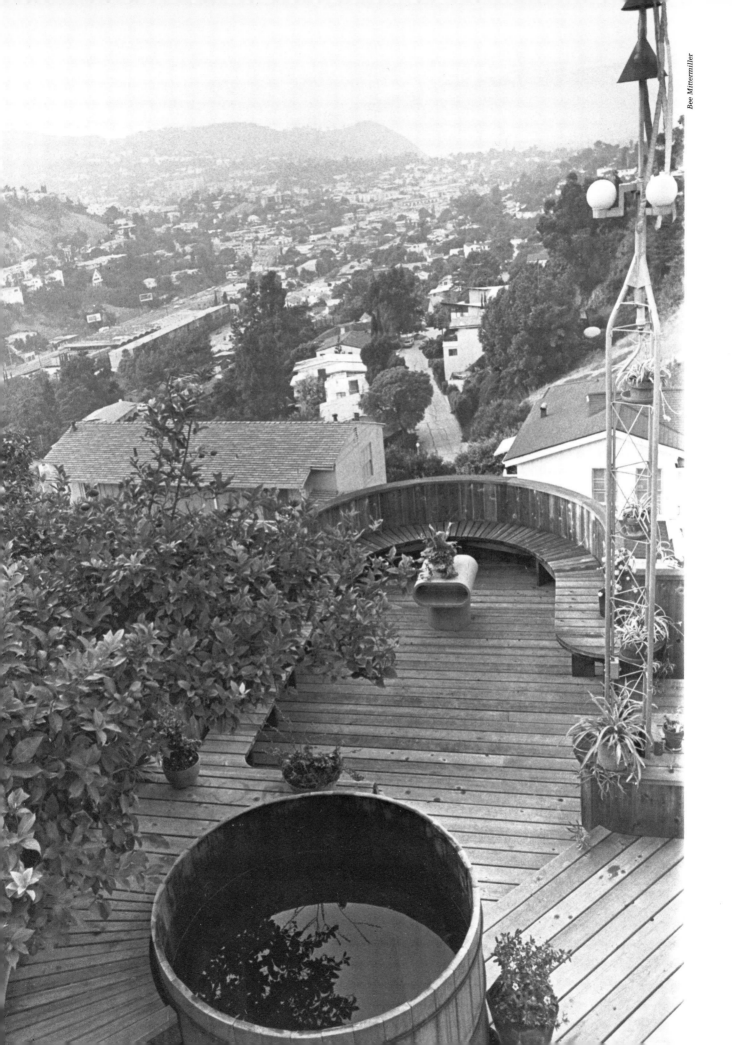

An Emphatic Extension

A new Great Hall gives focus to a typically agglomerated house in Connecticut.

PROJECT PROFILE
Connecticut residence
Location: Weston, Conn.
Architects: Shope Reno Wharton Associates
Budget: $85,000
Area renovated: 600 ft²
Area added: 640 ft²

Despite location, view, a charming centuries-old house, and 3½ rolling acres of prime real estate, the new owners of a miniature estate in Connecticut sensed that two things were missing.

The first was easy enough to envision— a swimming pool. The second dissatisfaction was far more vague and visceral. Despite its rambling sweetness, their new antique home lacked a coherent identity. The owners sensed that a special space was needed, for although the convoluted form of the house possessed charm, history, and even wit, there was no graceful place providing a spiritual center for the entire estate.

Connecticut Yankees are nothing if not industrious. When there is a task to be done, it is done with vigor (if not always with enough thought). So it was with this house of many pieces. The original barn was 230 years old, and over the last 150 years additions, revisions, and aesthetic collisions had left a charming hodgepodge of formal variation, rhythm, and scale.

Unfortunately, activity without purpose or rest is both meaningless and exhausting. Of this house's many parts, none was ever originally designed as a home. At some point one barn joined another, and the subsequent extra spaces blurred their distinction and extended the overall mass. But with all this space and structure there was no heart, no dominant space, or in the tradition of New England homes, no massive hearth to signal the family center.

The owners called in a young architecture firm from nearby Greenwich, Shope Reno Wharton Associates. Perhaps emboldened by their youth, the architects were not intimidated by the two centuries of uncontrolled growth that they encountered.

The clients, native New Yorkers, wanted the luxury of a grand space, perhaps in response to the urban labyrinths they were endeavoring to escape. In response, the architects extruded an existing gable profile some 40 feet to the west, enclosing a clear span space 20 feet wide and 20 feet high at the peak.

For some that would have been fantasy enough and the extended shape would have grown an antiqued skin—rather like a baby in a three-piece suit. But Shope, Reno, and Wharton saw the existing building for what it was: a patchwork of slightly different styles, all sheathed in white clapboard and capped with shingles but each distinct. The architects realized that the house was simply undergoing its latest quilting bee and their patch, though quite large, was nonetheless merely a piece of the composition.

Given the formal nature of the addition, a Classical bent was applied to the detailing. But the most expressive single feature of the project is also the least ambiguous— that is to say, the most overtly contemporary in style and image. The culmination of so much space and the vertical punctuation for the newly elongated form is the extraordinarily massive chimney.

Architects rarely get the chance to tinker with an 80-foot-long formal elevation. In the true spirit of Classical balance, the somewhat astounding chimney mass serves to offset the existing array of dormers and bay windows present on the opposing end of the facade.

Exterior compositional reasoning aside, the overtly dense mass of the chimney serves as the formal anchor for the entire house. The monolithic form does contain some crenelations, and a suitably scaled capping piece does add a modicum of formal articulation. But the essential architectural purpose of the chimney is to act in concert with the similarly aggrandized space of the new living room. The interplay of solid and void

OWNER'S STATEMENT

Why did we buy the house in Weston? Situated on three rural acres with a pond and stream only 70 minutes from New York and ten minutes from Long Island Sound, the old gardener's cottage cum barn, once a dependency of a 1751 New England house in Weston, Connecticut, met all our criteria for a refuge from the city. Easily accessible yet secluded, adequate in size yet not too large, the historically interesting house combined low-ceilinged cozy bedrooms and a library with a large living room. An easy place to entertain guests and family, it required only an architectural rehabilitation and the addition of the natatorium (to accommodate my husband's only form of physical exercise) to make it perfect.

ARCHITECTS' STATEMENT

The Weston, Connecticut, residence was pieced together during the last 150 years by joining together two nineteenth-century barns. The current owners purchased the property in 1982 and embarked on a major renovation and addition to the house. It was the owners' intention that the addition be designed in keeping with the warmth and scale of early New England architecture, and yet the purpose of the new addition was to create a sense of relief from the somewhat claustrophobic rooms in the original house. The inherent dichotomy between creating relief from the existing architecture and yet remaining visually consistent with that architecture became a challenge to the architects and was addressed with classical elements.
—*Shope Reno Wharton Associates*

H. Durston Saylor

fig. 1 *New elevation created as the combination of the existing (left) and the new (right). Note the crease in the siding at the point where new addition meets existing building.*

fig. 2 *Plan. A series of connected boxes sprouts a wing (right). Note the new entry portal to the far left and the new axis extending through the entire house. Note also the freestanding plan elements obscuring the full spatial impact until the living room is entered.*

Line drawing by the architects

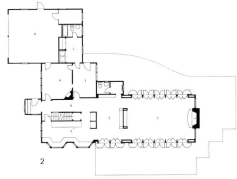

2

3

has been simplified to a nearly symbolic level in response to the detail-dissipated formal blur of the generating building. It would seem an aging beast has grown a head, and it is quite handsome.

The linkage to the main body of the original building is derived not merely from the simple formal extrusion defining its shape. The interior entry sequence has become a grand evolutionary vista that can prepare the entrant for the unprecedented spatial volume to come. A new entry box has been applied, and a hallway cleared of barriers and distractions to welcome and tease those entering the building.

In these manipulations can be seen the most radical departure from the New England sensibility. Doors, windows,

and fireplaces were the focal points of Colonial interior space because Colonial architecture was inherently an architecture of walls. In the new addition and in the retro-fitted entry sequence, the architecture of space becomes the overriding emphasis.

It is the straightforward approach to revision that makes this scheme exciting. The clear vision of the architects is reflected in the quality of space they have enclosed and in the extraordinary chimney form they have created.

Never mocking the parent building, Shope Reno Wharton Associates have transformed the old ensemble, once again. One can only hope that the next spate of building activity can maintain the stylistic evolution of the house with the success of this latest invigorating addendum.

4

fig. 3 *Living room interior. Tie beams (top) enable a clear span space, as the chimney orders their span. Note the minor variations on the chimney surface.*

fig. 4 *End view. The new chimney fairly dwarfs the building it serves.*

fig. 5 *New stair. Note the overscaled size of all the elements added by the architects, from newel post and spindles to extended wall at stair level to incorporate two risers and treads.*

fig. 6 *View upon entry. A great axis rewards the viewer with a vista to remember. Note the ceiling perforation at upper right. Note also the bright living room beckoning beyond the smaller intermediate spaces.*

5

6

Upwardly Mobile

*Building upon a basic bungalow, Martin Henry
Kaplan has made a forgotten building
a thing to remember.*

Martin Henry Kaplan is an architect in Seattle, Washington. Despite his training and experience, it was not so much the architecture he purchased when he bought a 1920s in-city "Seattle Bungalow" as it was the view and the air rights that went with it. From Kaplan's little house sitting on a tiny lot atop Queen Anne Hill, there is a 225° unobstructed view of downtown Seattle. Fortunately, the house sat on the south-facing slope of the hill, providing a perfect site for an energy-efficient house.

Essentially the existing structure was an 820-square-foot two-bedroom house sitting on a garage. The living room was all of 10 feet wide, while the major circulation corridor for the house ran through the kitchen (which was all of 5 feet wide). In short, this was a house of tiny rooms wedged onto a tight lot. It was obvious that decongestion was only possible in the vertical direction. But rather than simply add another floor and divide the square footage to accommodate new rooms, Kaplan opted to create an event.

The backbone of any vertical addition is the means of access, the stair. Kaplan located his circulation spine on the northern, backyard side of the house.

The spatial intention of the addition that fed off the stair was simple: move bedrooms to the new second floor to create a living area on the first floor that was indeed bigger than the proverbial bread box. Then Kaplan further liberated the site's limitations by creating a "backyard" in the sky, a rooftop deck capturing the view once only guessed at.

The method by which these moves were realized involved two basic exterior manip-

---

PROJECT PROFILE

Kaplan residence
Location: Seattle, Wash.
Architect: Martin Henry Kaplan
Budget: Not available
Area renovated: 1320 ft^2
(including garage)
Area added: 700 ft^2
(not including deck)

**OWNER-ARCHITECT'S
STATEMENT**

I wanted to expand interior public zones and maximize views and solar-assisted energy efficiencies. Limited zoning restrictions and requirements suggested a strong vertical plan articulation organized into zones for environmental control and related to passive and active heat distribution and natural cooling through a directed vertical air flow. The building envelope utilizes available insulating materials designed and installed to potentially eliminate air infiltration and reduce associated heat loss. I also wanted to reduce window-to-wall area, eliminate northern fenestration except for ventilators, and create a building envelope that provided a platform for an in-city "yard" on the rooftop maximizing views and privacy—an amenity required by limited site dimension and juxtaposition to neighboring houses.
—*Martin Henry Kaplan*

---

ulations. First, adding to the house with a Modernist method of geometry—a rectilinear wall system, emphasizing broad planes and directly expressed spatial volumes growing out of the existing mass. Second, wrapping this hybrid of old and new, roofs and walls, in a cedar-shingle blanket to unify and soften the effect of the addition.

To liberate tight spots in the plan (such as the accommodation of a closet or bath), saddlebag-style bays were attached to the basic existing plan outline. Similarly, the form of the vertical extension demurred from the original building's perimeter by holding its mass away from the street side of the house, thus mitigating the impact of the addition on the street.

The result is a wholly new building whose new forms grow directly out of the existing bungalow, without the overt evidence of anything more than a natural growth of form taking place. All of this done while keeping the code-required 35-foot height limitation.

Capping the building's vertical ascent into the architecture of the 1980s, a cantilevered frame hangs above the outline of the triumphant crow's nest. Like the exclamation point at the end of a protracted sentence, the effect of this hovering white datum is a welcome surprise.

As well as envisioning a view, Martin Kaplan saw the energy present in the air above his bungalow, the energy realized when an existing structure is transformed into a new entity. Besides capturing views of Puget Sound, the Cascade and Olympic mountains, and Mount Rainier, Kaplan succeeded in capturing, and holding, our imagination as well.

1

2

fig. 1 *The realized project. New windows and siding and the three-story massing transform the bungalow into a sculptured object. Kaplan extended the plane of the east facade up into the new floor and created a secondary extended vertical plane following the existing line of the eastern back porch. The new plane becomes dominant in the addition's massing and culminates in the boxlike deck structure at the uppermost level. The final gesture toward the sky, the cantilevered frame, achieves a final disintegration of the bungalow.*

fig. 2 *The existing house. Almost prototypical of the Seattle Bungalow, the 1926 house had the standard subsequent modifications of deck, railing, and picture-window. Note that both entries and the foundation remain unchanged in the final project.*

Photos and line drawings by the architect

fig. 3 *Bird's-eye view. A kinetic mass of shingles amid the bungalows on Queen Anne Hill.*

fig. 4 *Living room interior. Where the roof is unaffected by the additional floor, Kaplan raised the ceiling to the underside of the roof rafters. The flat ceiling under the addition helps define the kitchen area in the open plan. Note the stepped skylights and new firebox.*

3

5

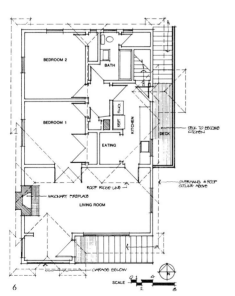

6

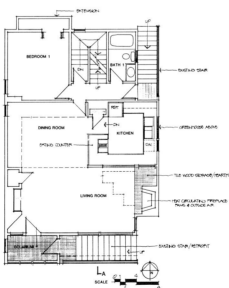

fig. 5 *Crow's nest. The final realization of a vertically developing mass, this serves as a "backyard" on a tight site, and the view achieved is a rare amenity. The cantilevered frame serves as a formal culmination to the massing from the street but captures the view and defines a room in the unlimited expanse of sky.*

fig. 6 *Original (left) and revised (right) plans. The basic intention of the addition project was to provide adequate living space. This was accomplished in three ways. First, two bedrooms were moved upstairs (leaving a single bedroom on the first floor). Second, Kaplan simply eliminated all interior walls in the southern two-thirds of the house. Last, the kitchen was extended to the east (enclosing an existing deck), and "saddlebag" additions for a closet and a fireplace were similarly extended. An interesting aside in relocating the fireplace: The architect recycled the removed brick as flooring for the new southern greenhouse.*

Bared Essentials

By eliminating all unnecessary partitions and extending a deck, Wiebenson & McInturff, Architects, destroy the limits of a typical Cape Cod house.

PROJECT PROFILE

Evans residence
Location: Washington, D.C.
Architects: Wiebenson & McInturff, Architects
Budget: $40,000
Area renovated: 700 ft^2
Area added: 400 ft^2 (deck only)

Mary Evans knew that the space her house afforded just did not suit her needs. She also knew that the solution was quite simple, to remove a wall or two and relocate the kitchen to a larger existing space.

If the extent of her perceptions ended at that point, she could have found the name of a builder in the phone book and all the necessary moves could have been effected with a minimum of thought. It is to her delight that Mary Evans sensed that a gratuitous gut-and-paste remodeling job would only address the rudimentary problems of immediate need and obvious misfit. She acted on her intuition by calling Wiebenson & McInturff, a local Washington, D.C., architectural firm.

It was obvious to the architects that simply removing walls would have left several large problems. First of all, the primary focus of Mary Evans's frustration was the major wall bisecting the house in the long direction. John Wiebenson and Mark McInturff realized that the offending partition concealed heating ducts and provided the major internal support for the house; hence, a simple gutting of the interior space could prove quite costly. Second, the Cape Cod-style house had the prototypically centered front door dividing a modest house into two equal (and undersized) areas. Last, the house itself lacked any tangible sense of vitality. When spending tens of thousands of dollars, a home owner hopes to purchase more than basic spatial accommodation, even though that was essentially what Mary Evans was asking for.

The architects took up the challenge of selective rejection of partitions where possible, leaving those elements that would prove too costly to move, which included the stair, the half bath, the heating-ducts, and the exterior form of the house itself.

OWNER'S STATEMENT

Not until after the remodeling was I aware that space could reflect aesthetic values as well as meet practical needs. Initially, I decided to remodel for purely practical reasons, but, by the final stages, I realized that the whole house had undergone a transformation that also reflected my own aesthetic taste. I used to have to adapt myself to the space of the house both functionally and aesthetically; now, the space is completely adapted to my needs—the perfect marriage of function and form, and a never-ending source of pleasure.—*Mary Evans*

ARCHITECTS' STATEMENT

We approached the house as if we were carving away the unnecessary pieces rather than adding necessary ones. Most of the walls on the first floor were opened up or removed. Those parts of walls that contained important structural or mechanical systems were retained, since the budget did not allow for major revisions of those systems.

Mary Evans continues to enjoy her house, and we continue to work on it. We are just completing some furniture for the living and dining rooms, and work is beginning on the garden. After that, there is always the second floor, a beach house, or . . .
—*Mark McInturff*

With those areas remaining in place, the architects moved the entry door to align with the gap between the existing bath and the remaining stair, creating a circulation axis that divided the house into a major part for socializing and a minor part for ancillary spaces of study, bath, and kitchen. In so doing, they created a visual axis as well, affording an expansive vista upon entry that would serve to lure the visitor to the newly developed backyard.

The architects could have simply decided that by removing the appropriate walls and relocating the entry and kitchen, they had done their job, and in the purest problem-solving sense, they had. But in attempting to remodel an existing home, architects cannot simply revise and refit. If architects are to give their client a complete service, it is their job to have a broad vision of what the best possible solution might be and then to work to revitalize the existing home with that ultimate image in mind.

Needless to say, the architects for this project realized that their piecemeal removal of expendable wall fragments left a hodgepodge of shapes and voids with nothing to organize them. In the best spirit of using responsive abstractions, Wiebenson and McInturff applied a system of horizontal banding that defined and related all the disparate remnants left over from their wall removal. Being a designed system rather than an arbitrary overlay, the horizontal layering generated new parts as well as organized existing pieces. The methods for this interior integration were quite simple. On wall surfaces, new and old, ¾-inch half-round molding was applied. This is possibly the least expensive molding profile available, and the simple bull-nose edge is easily extended across voids in the wall in the form of fixed shelving, where ¾-inch-thick shelf stock is a standard item. As

fig. 1 *Living area, facing stair. Simultaneously generative and ordering, the half-round molding defines all vertical levels in the walls dealt with by the architects. The stair's imposition into the space is mitigated by the removal of most of its walls. The subtle tone progression from dark to light gray tones can be seen in the wall planes between the white molding. Note that the continuity of flooring also helps to simplify a potentially chaotic ensemble. All materials and methods used are unexceptional— only the results are extraordinary.*

fig. 2 *Axonometrics, before (left) and after (right). A cluttered box is transformed into an open, integrated series of spaces. Note the change in front door location (outline on lower right edge of both drawings). Note also that the location of the stair remains unchanged but its enclosing walls are minimized.*

Line drawings by the architects
Photos by Mark McInturff

1

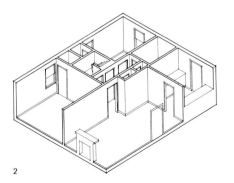
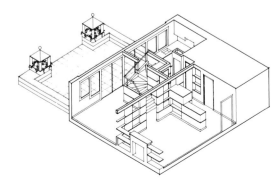

2

3

4

fig. 3 *Stair. Form, plane, space, and line act in a coherent concert to create a kinetic ensemble of parts where once only inert partitions existed. The consistent wood flooring and steps contrast with the wall system imposed on the affected surfaces. Similarly, the somewhat sinuous handrail is an applied element, distinct from either wall or floor system.*

fig. 4 *Cross axis. Taken from the point at which the circulation axis crosses the line of the bearing wall partially eroded by the architects' remodeling, this picture reveals a clarity of coordination. Note in the background the wall unaffected by the remodling, which remains unbanded.*

fig. 5 *Backyard. The newly opened up first floor opens invitingly to the new patio; note the stepped brick sills. The painted outline on the existing shingles alludes to the interior banding by being held back from the shingles' edge while its shape mirrors the pavilions created to terminate the flanking benches. All materials used are inexpensive, and the techniques employed are simple; hence, a major transformation is effected on a minor-league budget.*

5

well as wrapping and spanning, the motif was also employed to cap low wall elements. The architects added a sense of vitality to their layering with the use of progressively lighter gray tones painted between the white banding strips. The untouched and unbanded white walls contrast with the reworked walls and frame the new work done.

The overall effect is one of linear continuity amid the positive-negative interplay of partially removed walls—a Cartesian layer cake of lines and planes in concert.

The exterior treatment of the backyard similarly maximized the effect realized for the means available. The only added space is in the form of a patio. To bring the outside in, 80 percent of the first-floor back wall was replaced by sliding glass doors and windows. Flanking the sidelines of the patio paving, a low bench enclosure was installed, culminating in two miniature pavilions. The simple patio becomes a defined space captured by these elements rather

than just a spatial overflow from the house. By making this gesture to embrace the backyard and help connect it directly to the house, the architects create a focal point for the axis perceived upon entry to the house.

To finalize their happy impact on the existing exterior, the architects employed the cheapest of all remodeling materials—paint—on the shingled second-story facade above the new patio. Using a single color contrasting with the rest of the house, they transformed a mute shed-dormer facade into a whimsical skyline of architectural shapes.

It is when a budget meets ingenuity that talent is truly tested. It is relatively easy to create fantasy on a shoestring or a palace with unlimited resources. But when utility, economy, and delight emerge from the mundane confines of standard domestic architecture, it is an unqualified joy to behold. Mary Evans has the space she wanted, but more, she has the pride in ownership that comes with the laying on of hands.

Texas International

*A decaying Deco–Moderne–International Style
house in suburban Houston
gains new utility.*

An anonymous Texas family saw a home they admired at the 1938 world's fair in New York. Locating a set of plans, they returned home and proceeded to build the form most sincerely flattering to the original—a direct duplication.

Forty years had diluted this imitation's integrity with several shed additions and crude repairs of the normal wear and tear expected over such a span of time.

Richard and Barbara Calfee liked the neighborhood enough to buy the house despite the rather incongruous eastern urbanity of the International Style building set in the informal Texas suburbs. Somehow nautical, crisply stark, thoroughly sophisticated, the house was demeaned by the applied revisions previously mentioned. A sorry commentary on the proclivity of the average addition to be blind to the building it services, these addenda served to galvanize the resolve of the Calfees to rekindle the naive purity of form their house once had.

But these awkward additions had addressed some very real inadequacies of the original house plan. So the Calfees sought not only to preserve their curious abode's unique styling but also to bring the functional utility of the house up to the standards of the present generation of suburban home owners.

Essentially, the needs were to increase the living space, to design space to accommodate special activities and storage, and to create a master bedroom suite. The major formal and functional emphasis was on the new living room spaces the Calfee family required. It seemed obvious that these new spaces should relate to a large tree that dominated the backyard but went unrecognized by the existing house's massing and orientation.

The Calfees realized they had to double the usable square footage of their home and yet retain all the stylistic peculiarities that helped charm them into purchasing it in the first place. With a similar faith in first impressions, the Calfees contacted Wm. T.

PROJECT PROFILE

Calfee residence
Location: Houston, Tex.
Architects: Wm. T. Cannady &
Associates, Inc.
Budget: Not available
Area renovated: 400 ft^2
Area added: 450 ft^2
(including master bedroom)

OWNER'S STATEMENT

People have told us our house looks like a boat. We call it 1939 Moderne or International Art Deco. We came to appreciate its unique qualities. We liked the neighborhood's trees and age and the fact that it was well-settled (and the houses didn't all look the same).

We wanted to stay with this kind of house, whatever it is. We didn't want to put on anything that didn't belong.

The result was a much more efficient use of the space we had. We economized by agreeing to paint the old rooms ourselves.

—*Barbara Calfee*

ARCHITECTS' STATEMENT

The current owners wanted to resalvage the house while adding a family room on the ground floor and enlarging the master bedroom on the second floor to include a study, more storage space, and a new bath.

The solution began with removing the two delapidated and unusable structures not original to the design and replacing them with more harmonious elements.

On the east, the addition opens up the previously closed dining and living rooms in a light-filled circuit that focuses on a commanding live oak. Above, the study occupies the most prominent tree-viewing corner with an equal expanse of shaded glass.

—*Wm. T. Cannady
& Associates, Inc.*

Cannady & Associates, architects, on the basis of the attractive quality of their offices, which they had encountered by chance.

Luckily both impetuous decisions combined to create a delightful extension of a bygone Futurist aesthetic into the realm of contemporary utility.

Once the clumsy tack-ons were ripped off, the remaining form was a simple rectangular box with a rounded corner cum entry. The architects had to take an architectural fait accompli and devise a system for indiscernible growth.

Obviously, materials and detailing were to be duplicated in whatever addition was effected. Roof, eave, and window heights would be aligned. To simply extend the existing box would create a scaleless and boring volume that would be a cosmetic application of the given motifs encountered.

Instead the architects opted to animate their addition with some subtle stepping of the massing. Cannady & Associates created a rounded corner recognizing the dominant tree behind the house by mimicking the entry corner previously noted.

In several quiet ways the architects manipulated the existing aesthetic to open up the house to the outside world and create a less formal ambience. Shaded northerly glazing was clustered to the point of creating window walls to the backyard, complete with French doors. Exterior walls were extended to define a deck. A fireplace flue runs up on an outside wall and punctures the eave with a suppressed irreverence. These respectfully unprecedented architectural evolutions all face the backyard, maintaining the formality of the street-facing facade.

The resulting building is as thoroughly true to the original design as was the existing building to its world's fair precedent, and yet the architects have evolved its essence into a new home affording the amenities that were once impossible.

1

2

fig. 1 *Backyard view. Away from public eyes, the rear portion of the addition creates an unprecedented amount of glazing and rear-yard access. Note the flue to upper left and deck to lower left.*

fig. 2 *Exterior from the street. The restored existing portion of the house is to the left, with the addition in the right background. Note the duplicate corner window.*

Photos by Paul Hester

4

5

fig. 3 (opposite) *Sidestepping. A simple stepping of the new addition form quietly defines the old-new interface. Note the identical detailing.*

fig. 4 *Living room interior. The new glazing creates an open, informal ambience. Note how the quarry-tile floor extends to create the hearth and frame the firebox.*

fig. 5 *Addition. Identical detailing and materials, with aligned eave and window heights, create a rational extension of the existing building that allows for the subtle deformation of the house as it wraps around to the backyard. Note the low walls, centered on the focal tree.*

A Tudor Touch

Kent Bloomer softens a stark house in Connecticut.

PROJECT PROFILE

Downey residence
Location: Guilford, Conn.
Designer: Kent Bloomer,
assisted by Kimo Griggs
Budget: $5000
Area renovated: 300 ft^2
Area added: 120 ft^2 (interior)
200 ft^2 (deck)

Dr. Wayne Downey is a psychiatrist. As his private practice developed, it became clear that he had to redirect the pedestrian traffic flow around his home.

Several years ago Joan and Wayne Downey designed the existing building dealt with in this article. Consulting with a builder, they lavished attention on the plan layout of the house to the point where it perfectly met their needs. Unfortunately, the process of design ended at that stage. Without much attention being paid to the exterior form of the building, the plans were given to the builder for his implementation.

As you might expect, the built form was as simple as a builder could make it. The visual image thus created was bereft of those elements of detail, scale, and massing that can transform a utilitarian plan into responsive architecture.

So when Dr. Downey contacted designer Kent Bloomer in an effort to resolve the circulation problems, the good doctor knew that there was another level of design that had to be addressed in whatever solution was effected.

Bloomer, a professor at Yale, approached the problem with a firm grasp of architectural history and the hands-on experience of an accomplished sculptor. The functional problems of family-client segregation seemed complex but not overwhelming. Incoming patients had to know which entrance to use from the street, while exiting patients had to have their own distinct and separate way out, and the Downey family had to preserve its own entrance and privacy. These problems were solved quite early in the planning process. A clear mind can effectively deal with two-dimensional problems, but it takes some formal ingenuity to translate the "best-laid plans" into rewarding aesthetics.

After careful consideration, office access

OWNER'S STATEMENT

This was originally a novice-designed dwelling emphasizing a harmonic internal layout for family activities. It was conceptualized as an organically developing structure to be modified as family needs changed. Appearance and "grounding" in the landscape were deemphasized in favor of interior vistas.

The recent modifications were prompted by a wish to have a professional psychiatric office at home surrounded by nature. A clear differentiation of family and professional areas had to be part of the new design. Increased energy efficiency was another priority. Integrating the building and its landscape and aesthetically refining its stark geometry were other goals.
—T. Wayne Downey, M.D.

DESIGNER'S STATEMENT

The principal new functions would fit the house physically but not architecturally. New signage governing entry had to be established, and domestic territory had to be segregated from the privy domain of patients without fracturing the visual unity of the house.

The solution was adding two English bays, an architectural element that in the country-house tradition generally held important interior functions. The domestic bay is identified by an arched entrance, while the larger and lower office bay stands beside a conventional door. Both bays collect solar energy.

The trellis then expands the composition laterally while giving a public-private character to the landscape.—*Kent Bloomer*

was located in the original garage entrance on the basement level, easily accessible from the street. While the existing house plan had located the family's entrance, Bloomer realized that a secluded exterior family space would facilitate domestic privacy from the ongoing traffic. By locating these critical areas, Bloomer had fixed the foci for his work.

It became obvious to the designer that such a blank box could serve as the perfect foil for some overtly ornamental gestures. The form and detailing of those gestures would have to enliven the house as a whole without insulting it. It became apparent that all the entries dealt with would employ screens of one sort or another to obscure direct visual access without creating the inhospitable implications of opaque walls.

In the absence of any discernible rhythms or visual patterns in the existing house, Bloomer realized his screens should have a life of their own. With a clear understanding of what was functionally and aesthetically desirable, Bloomer seized on a motif often employed in English country-house architecture—the progressively intricate glazing patterns of Tudor or Gothic bay windows. This seemingly arbitrary starting point was redefined by Bloomer and applied in a marvelously innocent manner.

Bloomer rectified and abstracted the historically curvilinear geometries to create a buildable motif that could be utilized in several conditions. First, the office needed a visual signal to the street of its entrance. By creating an air lock for the exit portal with his new pattern serving as the framework for the glazing, Bloomer keyed both professional portals with one element. Second, the back door used by the family needed both recognition and a means of creating a private area of the backyard. A wing wall and trellis incorporating the pattern were

1

fig. 1 *Rear entry. Once a solitary door flush with the wall, the entry now serves as both an air lock and a light well to the renovated basement. The lattice (left) shields a new deck.*

Line drawing by the designer
Photos by Kimo Griggs

fig. 2 *Existing house. Drawn in a style faithful to the depth of complexity present in the architecture encountered, Bloomer's sketch conveys the starkly mute image of an unexamined exterior.*

fig. 3 *The revised result. The blank box becomes bejeweled. The counterpoint created adds life and purpose to the inert mass dealt with. The back door is at left, and the new office bay is at right.*

fig. 4 *Deck and lattice. Through the use of the new lattice, the old house, and nature's bounty, an exterior room is well defined.*

fig. 5 *Side view. At car level the office entrance is to the left of the new glazed bay. The discreet exit is contained in the bay's right end. Note that the suburban driveway has been transformed into a rusticated path.*

2

3

4

added, and beyond it a deck was built to allow for secluded outdoor living. Last, in creating a basement office, natural light had to be brought into a subterranean environment. Bloomer extended his new rear entry to include a light well with clerestory glazing framed by his energetic pattern.

In the same way fine jewelry can transform the image of a nondescript face, Bloomer's new elements recreate the image of a thoroughly mute building. By their overtly eccentric nature these semiabstracted constructions serve as sweet seasoning to a deadly dull exterior.

Ultimately these elements address the exterior inadequacies caused by the internal focus of the original building. A starkly utilitarian form is reincarnated by Bloomer, transformed into a two-part harmony of passive mass and active art.

5

Frosting on the Cake

Graham Gund converts an urban studio into a town house.

PROJECT PROFILE

Deutsch residence
Location: Boston, Mass.
Architect: Graham Gund
Budget: $64,000
Area renovated: 300 ft^2
Area added: 500 ft^2

Much to their delight, Ira and Margaret Deutsch had been able to convert a garage into a flat in downtown Boston. To have a freestanding home in a tightly packed urban neighborhood was quite a coup. But housing two adults, a car, bath, kitchen, bed, piano, and harpsichord within 900 square feet would challenge the most anal-retentive of home owners.

When time and money allowed, the couple decided to change the way their cramped quarters forced them to live. Music was a large part of their lives, and its practice and performance deserved its own separate space—as did the occasional guest who came to visit. However, their 900-square-foot house stood on an 1100-square-foot lot, affording little room for any expansion other than via a vertical addition.

The first step was to call in an architect. The Deutschs contacted Graham Gund.

What Gund encountered was the architectural yin just waiting to be made whole by an adorning yang. The original garage provided the foundation, while the later conversion provided the mechanical systems and bedroom space. In creating a new living room and kitchen, Gund would not only transform a studio into an urban house, he would create a crowning glory above the bald pate of single-story brick walls and flat roofing that stood nakedly on the site.

In urban New England the traditional styles of homes built in the last century dominate the residential areas of any given city. To go completely against that grain with an abstract Modernist mass suspended above the street would be foolish and awkward. But to tow the line and duplicate the adjacent buildings would reduce the design process to an act of photocopying the surrounding environs. Gund, however, saw the possibilities in creating a new building that makes sense of the old foundation.

Gund seized on the typically square plan of the original two-car garage portion of the

OWNER'S STATEMENT

Space was the major reason we decided to add onto our home.

It's a wholly new type of architecture from what existed before, when there was lots of exposed, dark wood. Now, with white plaster walls, and more windows and light, it feels totally different. I liked the house the way it was, but I like it even better now. When I go out to dinner, I can't wait to get home. To put a living room upstairs is wonderful.

Other homes on Beacon Hill are just gorgeous inside, but outside they are quite uniform. Our house is so distinctive. All the neighbors feel that the house enhances the area, and with Graham Gund using the materials he did, it fits into the neighborhood just beautifully.—*Margaret Deutsch*

ARCHITECT'S STATEMENT

The Deutsch house transforms what was originally a one-story, flat-roofed, two-car garage into a 2½-story house. Located on the "flat" of Beacon Hill, on a street visually cluttered with the back-end additions, fences, and parked cars of large Beacon Street town houses, the house was conceived as a freestanding pavilion above a garden wall.

Trellis-clad stucco walls and brick and wrought-iron elements reinforce the garden imagery. In an area where examples of Colonial, Federal, Neoclassical, and Victorian architecture all harmoniously coexist, we used traditional building materials and the Classical principle of symmetry to create a whimsical design that is both distinctive and yet appropriate to its context.—*Graham Gund*

existing building as his point of departure. He transformed that two-dimensional outline into its volumetric projection, a cube. The architect capped his classic shape with a celebratory roof, double-pitched to a flattened crown.

The resulting nonaxial form is the positive recognition of the house's street-corner siting, its form standing in singular celebration of its distinct identity as a freestanding urban house.

The classic exterior form is well seasoned by the applied trim detailing. The simple geometric window forms are framed by overwide trim that stands several inches proud of the stucco facade. Inserted behind the trim and covering the entire second-floor addition is an ornamental lattice. This grid seems to support and frame the windows, creating a lightly dynamic ambiguity between structure and ornament. Adding to the visual activity, the elements are color-coded in contrasting, though traditionally architectural, colors. The busy pattern of shadow, line, and color serves to add a dash of unexpected whimsy to a stoic Boston street.

With the new exterior form drawing the eye up from the pavement, the implicit promise of rewarded expectations had to be honored in the interior. With second-story living rooms, the trick for the architect is to create an entry that is sufficiently seductive to lure the visitors up a flight of stairs once they have entered the building.

Gund graced his entry with a kinetic custom stair and two mysterious columns. Untouched by the stair or ceiling, these white tubes ascend into a space that is only hinted at upon entry. Quite a departure from the predictable brick walls the visitor has just passed through, the effect is quite alluring.

The revealed space sits beneath the entire roof's bonnet, punctuated by gabled clerestory windows and a skylight or two.

1

fig. 1 *In a neighborhood of flat roofs, row houses, and unending brick buildings, Gund creates a minor landmark. A garage becomes a garden wall pediment for an assertive addition, redefining and celebrating the street corner. The abstracted trim detailing (including the custom gutter cum cornice) creates a lightly cartoonish effect in contrast to the serious surroundings.*

fig. 2 *Axonometric. Much more than an attic, the new second story atop a simple brick garage is a celebration of open space, classic massing, and dynamic detailing.*

Line drawing by the architect
Photos by Steve Rosenthal

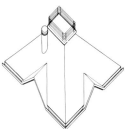

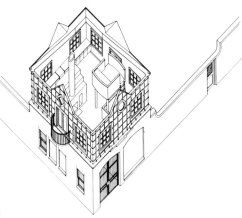

2

fig. 3 *Entry. An animated stair and naked columns teasingly invite the visitor to ascend into an open space as yet unseen. Note that the materials and detailing serve as a vignette of things to come.*

fig. 4 *Living room (from dining area). The freestanding objects create a landscaped space, defining areas, condensing various functions, and freeing up the perimeter walls and ceiling so they may serve as a simple enclosing envelope.*

fig. 5 *Living room interior. The crow's nest (right) sits above the head of the stairs, defining a transition space mediating between the stair, the living area, and the dining area. Note the stiffening beam connecting the construction to the wall. To the left the stepped mass condenses a multitude of functions and serves to obscure the new kitchen. The double doors in the center background lead to a deck atop a wing of the existing studio.*

3

4

5

The nonfocused space gains meaning and scale by the objects designed to sit in it. The entry columns, so mysteriously distinct from the building's structure, are exposed to be the supports for a nook in the sky, or crow's nest containing a desk. Gund also condenses fireplace, speakers, and kitchen cabinets and appliances into a stepped mass resting sedately on the floor. The stalactite-stalagmite identities in clear counterpoint, these constructions mediate between the large scale of the enveloping space and the scale of the furniture around them. Second, these objects serve to define subspaces, eliminating the need for ordinary walls and doors. The perimeter walls and ceiling are freed of the attachments that might serve to limit the sense of expansiveness that exists without them.

A simple Modernist vernacular of manipulated white planes and oak trim and flooring serves as the common denominator to all this activity. This continuity of surface treatment allows furniture and art to stake their own claims for appreciation without competition from the architecture that houses them.

The merit of this project lies in its creative denial of the drab urban environment it sits in. The animated exterior detailing, freestanding form, and effervescent interior all stand in happy contrast to the city sensibilities the average urban dweller has been lead to expect. More than an island of excitement in a sea of brick and blacktop, this addition gives its prosaic plinth a meaning never envisioned by its owners.

Shingled Showpiece

Susana Torre adorns a Southampton, New York, carriage house with elements that both redefine and reinforce its latent charm.

PROJECT PROFILE

Clark Residence
Location: Southampton, N.Y.
Architect: Susana Torre,
The Architecture Studio
Budget: $72,660
Area renovated: 2000 ft^2
Area added: 870 ft^2

In 1910 a carriage house for an estate in Southampton was often a sweet dessert for the architect after he had gorged himself on a massive and complex mansion for some captain of industry. Grosvenor Atterbury, the 1910 equivalent of a jet-set architect, had the pleasure of designing this perfect little box, and until Joseph S. Clark, Jr., needed a scaled-down summer house, it had only one revision—the horses it housed were replaced by automobiles.

Being an outbuilding, the structure was not sited for any amenity other than convenience, so Joseph Clark had the vision to move the structure a quarter of a mile to a hilltop facing the water. It is at this stage of events that the focus of attention must turn to Susana Torre, the New York architect Clark retained to refit the carriage house, and the shell she encountered.

The building itself was bilaterally symmetrical, with two opposing end gables and two corresponding gable dormers. The corners were columnar, and the roof eave carried around all walls, recessing the first-floor end-gable walls. Essentially, the first floor was an open garage and the second was a servant's quarters.

Torre saw that the basic structure had to retain its integrity and yet the new use and siting had to be accommodated. She made three basic changes.

1. The spatial organization of the two floors was swapped: the open garage on the first floor was divided into bedrooms, while the previously subdivided attic became an open living area, its height providing a platform for amazing views.

2. Rather than civilize the landscape around the house, the architect extended a deck from the house to allow for summer socializing. This deck had to have easy access to the second-floor living area.

3. Since horses and cars were the pri-

OWNER'S STATEMENT

The carriage house has provided me with more pleasure and feelings of creativity than any art form I have ever seen (or lived in). It is the aerie of my childhood, with nooks and hidden branches and rooftops that take me back to my youth. It is also a growing art form; every day I see new aspects of its symmetry and assymmetry echoed in forms (circles and angles). As with any great art form, I never tire of it and always learn from it.
—*Joseph S. Clark, Jr.*

ARCHITECT'S STATEMENT

This is a modern house, a modern house whose point of departure is an existing architectural object, one that had grace, integrity, and elegance—and rather more character than refinement. I never really tried to be "correct" in the renovation. The manipulations between old and new take place in the so-called interface where the house by Atterbury touches the house by Susana Torre. Obviously, there had to be some elements in common to both the Shingle Style and the modern house. One of them is the overscaled arched window. It produces a transparency of space that is actually quite modern, but at the same time the shape of that window does relate to what we understand as the Shingle Style.—*Susana Torre*

mary concern when Atterbury designed the carriage house, Torre had to create a new entry. Given her second-story living room, the entry had to draw the visitor not only in but up as well.

These three changes all served to create an amazing interplay between the antique space, skin, and structure that were restored and the modern symbolism and spatial flow that was imposed on the building.

The entry and stair, once afterthoughts relegated to a convenient corner, have become events. Located by the aforementioned gable dormers on the transverse axis of the house, the new entry is boldly pronounced by a two-story lattice cum architectural symbol and sculpture. Overtly held off the house mass, the lattice facade supports a deck above, providing preliminary enclosure at the point of entry. Inside, the slot of space given over to entry is completely sheathed in the pine beaded tongue-and-groove siding so typical in Shingle Style summer-house interiors. The focus of the space and of the siding seams is the stair accessing the living area above. The exterior response to this focus is the second grand-scale element overlayed on the building by Torre—a huge glazed opening filling the gable dormer and culminating in a fixed fan window. At the half level of the stair, yet another deck affords easy penetration of the shingle skin. The stair terminates on the second floor at the cross axis of the opposing gable elements. The deck, which provided shelter at ground level, now provides a spatial release as one enters the living room.

The grand payoff to this manipulative sequencing is the liberated attic living room. The pine surfacing is as ubiquitous on the interior as the shingles are on the exterior surface of the building. The multifocused

1

fig. 1 *Southwest view. The bowed upper deck springs from the existing eave overhang. The new deck skirt and fan window clearly announce the new incarnation of an old building.*

fig. 2 *In transit. A tractor pulls a truck pulls a shingled mass to its new home.*

Line drawings by the architect

2

3

fig. 3 *Living room interior, facing kitchen. The new kitchen and bath are condensed and encapsulated by an overtly new wall, a blank facade kept distinct from the ubiquitous pine finish surface. Note that the brick flue remains, cleaned and exposed with unassuming honesty.*

fig. 4 *Floor plans showing the realized scheme. The new slot of entry space can be clearly seen on the first floor (top). The wraparound deck touches the house only at the points of access. The second floor (bottom) has its vaulted space released by decks placed to visually extend the axes of the ceiling peaks.*

fig. 5 *Stair and fan window. Nighttime darkness creates a reflection of the living area opposite the window. Note the animated rail and distinct stair riser and tread edge.*

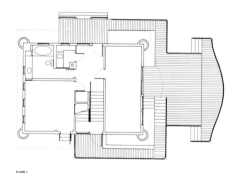

FLOOR I

142   **LIVING ROOMS AND FRONT DOORS**

4

5

grand-scale space dominates all the elements within it. The new kitchen and bath are condensed and isolated behind an interior facade of blank gypsum wallboard—again a symbolic facade evoking the interior-exterior ambiguity of the other Torre-inserted elements. Opposing the kitchen and serving as the cockpit or wheelhouse for the house is the small bowed deck, a simple extension of the existing eave-generated overhang mentioned before. The view from this focal point is awesomely unlimited.

Spreading beneath this crow's nest is the last major feature applied to the house by Torre, the large social deck. Carefully held away from the columnar corners, and touching the house only at points of access, the deck is centered on the house and bows its leading edge in response to the major end-gable axis. When the deck ascends to the half

level mentioned, it is surrounded by a vertically sided skirt hiding the awkward underside view created by its levitation. Secondly, the skirt and painted tubular steel rails create a distinctly new image.

The contrast between old house and new elements only serves to venerate the existing carriage house. By scaling her new elements as major parts of the renovated structure, Torre creates a dynamic between her vision and the unbowed innocent elegance of Atterbury's original box. By orienting these new pieces to the existing axes and by deriving their materials and forms from historical precedents in tune with the period of original construction, the architect allows the applied parts to transform the house without distressing its latent dignity.

     Timothy Hursley

fig. 6 *Elevations. The newly applied lattice wall and outsized fan window can be readily seen. The new deck is kept clearly distinct from the original house form.*

fig. 7 *View to south. From the new second-story bowed deck, the rolling hills finally give way to the ocean beyond.*

fig. 8 *Entry. A generous foyer focuses on the ascending stair.*

fig. 9 *Entry at night. The large form, scaled to relate to the existing building's size, serves to beckon the visitor with a transparent link to the interior.*

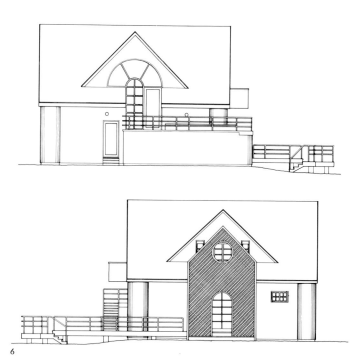

6

8   *Timothy Hursley*

A Sound Design

A retreat on New York's Long Island expresses its natural focus under the artful touch of Turner Brooks and Stuart Hamilton.

Coming from Vermont, Turner Brooks and his partner, Stuart Hamilton, were more than casually impressed with the serene prospect afforded the home they were commissioned to remodel. The uninterrupted view of Long Island Sound from an elevated posture was obviously exquisite. What was not obvious was the potential present in the motley Shingle Style house perched on a bluff overlooking the water.

Formally, the oblong building presented its short end toward the big view. Although the landlubber facade retained its early twentieth-century charm, years of revisionist construction to the water end of the house obscured any resemblance it had to its original form.

Appearing to be a collage of lumberyard and hardware-store catalog components, these applied decks, porches, and shed roofs of dimensional lumber and corregated fiberglass presented a vision of all that is ugly in ad hoc expansion. Beneath these unseemly scales, the original body of the house was essentially untouched.

Rather than reject the existing jumble of elements as chaotic and arbitrary, the architects divined the difference between the original eccentric charm of the house and the more recently applied grotesqueries mentioned. As an anonymous mechanic once said, "If it ain't broke, don't fix it," so Brooks and Hamilton left the northerly land-facing end of the house untouched. But the southerly end, long the butt of so many well-intentioned malaprops, was wiped clean of all those offending tack-ons.

While bold, these actions were obvious necessities to even the casual observer. What makes this addition so extraordinary is the way the architects knitted their new elements into the reconstituted fabric of the building they dealt with.

Although the existing additions removed were awkward at best, the needs they addressed were not lost to Brooks and Hamilton. The applied porches created enclosed space facing the view, extending far beyond the narrow confines of the existing building. Similarly the several sun-room additions brought light into the dim living spaces facing the water. An exterior stair allowed for access to the water. A second-story porch created an outdoor room for contemplating the water beyond. All of these removed elements were reincarnated by Turner Brooks and Stuart Hamilton.

The architects extended a single water-facing covered porch from the narrow southern end of the house. Secondly, they created the spatial response to the view so long ignored by the house they encountered. Essentially, the architects' design gutted the southern end of the building's interior, creating a single large living room facing the south.

Again Brooks and Hamilton, by providing space to address a dramatic view, did what any competent designers might do. But in their method of realizing their intentions, they display a rare aesthetic vision.

The architects utilize several long-span composite beams to carry the load of the floor above the newly gutted living room. By collecting the loading in this way, they can liberate the form of the newly extended south wall. The wall is designed to be an arcing plane bulging toward the sound, with its center point the existing entry into the room from the north end of the house. By orienting the new wall in this manner, the architects create an axis, and then they extend this axis with an almost monumental exterior stair, providing the direct access to the water missing in the original house. Following this axial orientation, Brooks and Hamilton further utilize their new heavy beaming in the living room ceiling to can-

1

2

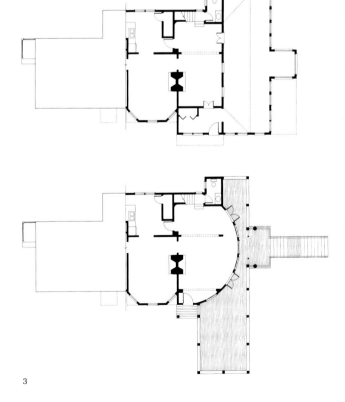

fig. 1 *The realized scheme. All the elements of the architects' design are evident in this view from the southwest. A new covered porch provides a shaded vantage point from which to view the water. A new stair descends to the sea, while above, the cantilevered deck and popped-out window bay reinforce the southern axis. Lurking behind all of these addenda, the curving, painted living room wall billows into the porch, centered on the stair.*

fig. 2 *Existing house. Shrouded in decks, lean-to roofs, and sun porches, the original house form is almost invisible.*

fig. 3 *First-floor plans. The existing first-floor plan (top) shows the wraparound sun porches surrounding the existing south facade. Not shown are the open porches extending to the west. In the revised plan (bottom) the new south wall seems to balloon toward the southerly sound. The newly created porch is subdivided by the bulge into major, minor, and access areas. Note how the stairs and the bath remain unchanged, saving a great deal of the construction budget for better purposes.*

3

Photos and line drawings by Turner Brooks

fig. 4 *Distant prospect. The newly realized scheme presents a profile similar to the one encountered with the existing conditions, but the consistency and ordering of parts has been clearly orchestrated by Brooks and Hamilton.*

fig. 5 *Master bedroom bay windows and deck. A minor counterpart to the bulging wall beneath it, this bay reaches to the water and has the new deck as its horizontal extension.*

fig. 6 *The stair. Gable, deck, curving wall, and unseen bay window align with these steps to provide an overriding orientation for both old and new aspects of the realized scheme. Note how the unprecedented Classical columns signal the newness of the applied stairs.*

fig. 7 *Exterior living room wall. With curving and painted clapboards amid the angular shingled forms, this inserted building form seems to inflate toward the sea.*

fig. 8 *Living room interior. Only the curvilinear form and expansive spatial quality of this room key its new status. Otherwise, moldings, windows, materials, and surface treatments are extensions of the building vernacular encountered. Note how an original wall fragment has been isolated by the new spatial expansion to become a column. Unseen in the ceiling cavity are two major composite wood beams collecting the loading of the floor and cantilevered deck above.*

7

8

tilever a second-story deck over the head of the new stair. The architects open up the vista for the second floor with a bay window extension of the existing master bedroom onto the newly created deck.

All of these new formal events are stylistically assimilated into the existing house by the extension of the existing shingle siding to wrap around all the surfaces created and encountered. There is one notable exception to this monomaterial skin treatment. The new curvilinear living room wall, so unprecedented in exterior form and in the interior spatial quality it defines, becomes a painted surface bulging toward the sound and safely nestled under the protective confines of the new porch.

As an architect, it is often all too easy to reject the mistakes of others and the follies of the past and assert a personal vision. In the art of designing an addition, this kneejerk revisionism can prove disastrous. Turner Brooks and Stuart Hamilton saw how the unfortunate additions they encountered accommodated and framed the exquisite view. They also saw the genuine charm of the original building that lay dormant under the applied confusion of subsequent additions.

By creating an axis to the sea, Brooks and Hamilton introduced an order lacking in the existing house. By providing the space required to apprehend such a magnificent view, they created the formal, functional, and spiritual heart for a home sorely in need of a tender vision.

THE COMPLETE OVERHAUL

When time, siting, or decay demand, existing homes must be thoroughly reworked if they are to be recycled. When bulldozing and building anew are not the answer, economics and contextual sensibilities dictate a responsive interplay between the bones that remain and the flesh to be applied.

INTRODUCTION

When prospective home owners read the words "Handyman Special" in the less than frank realtor's description of an existing home for sale, they are torn between excitement over the affordable price tag and fear of a potentially agonizing salvage project. The image that is conjured up by that descriptive phrase ranges from a collapsing barn to a sound home visually polluted by neglect. The raw material offered to the purchaser has all the physical limitations of an existing structure and all the headaches of a protracted building project.

What recommends these risky undertakings? First of all, the economics are frequently alluring. At the very least, the septic system, utility hookups, and foundation are usually adequate for reuse, and the price of these neglected relics is only marginally more than the cost of a naked building lot. Second, the location of older homes is frequently advantageous. The influx of affluence into an existing working-class area due to natural amenity or proximity to an urban center can create instant bargains where once good money might have been thrown after bad. Last, the latent charm of a battered building can shine poignantly through the thoughtless remodeling and rampant decay of its recent history.

It takes a special courage and vision to undertake a complete renewal of a desperately distressed structure. Often only an architect can see the latent promise and will serve as the owner-renovator. Frequently such projects do not make sense given the extreme cost of reconstruction, and only an engineer, architect, or competent builder can divine the hidden early warning signs of irretrievable decay.

Given the high risk and high reward implicit in the undertaking of these projects, it is best to maintain a firm grip on the origins of each of the examples shown in this section. It is all too easy to view such work as a new home built on an old foundation.

Frequently the architect must anguish over the real economies of what can be saved and what must be rebuilt. To surgically reweave selected portions of a partially defective structure can cost several times as much as a simple gut-and-rebuild approach. On the other hand, deciding to restructure an existing building completely when there is adequate structure in place does not make economic sense.

In a sense, these projects represent the broadest test of an architect's skill and knowledge. He has the freedom to express himself without the powerful presence of an existing building demanding his respect and attention as it can in the projects shown in previous chapters. And yet, the complete success of a major overhaul depends on the designer's genuine knowledge of the existing context in which the structure exists, so the designer's criteria for success are multiplied.

The judicious utilization of the viable parts of an existing building must be balanced with the essential reason for hiring an architect for such a project: that in solving practical dilemmas he can also maintain and enhance a creative vision beyond the myriad minutiae screaming for attention.

Mirrored Imagery

*Paul Bierman-Lytle transforms
a shed into a showcase.*

PROJECT PROFILE

Bierman-Lytle residence
Location: Guilford, Conn.
Designer: Paul Bierman-Lytle
Budget: Phase I, $15,000
       Phase II, $30,000
Area renovated: 300 ft²
Area added: Phase I, 400 ft²
       Phase II, 400 ft²

When Jane and Paul Bierman-Lytle located their first home, it was in the form of a small, rented, renovated outbuilding in the remains of an orchard.

When Jane became pregnant, Paul realized that their present comfy home would soon be cramped. He reacted as only a designer-builder working on his own home might.

Their civilized shack faced an even less imposing structure, a 300-square-foot freestanding library designed around some transplanted bookcases, long untouched by their landlord. Instead of moving to a new section of town or destroying the rustic simplicity of their first abode, the Bierman-Lytles looked to their awkward neighbor to embrace their growing family.

The lines of the outbuilding were simple enough and the materials were identical to the other structures around and in the orchard. It was decided that as a family grows by increments, so would this little structure, and the occupant-designer devised a two-phase approach.

The first need was to create a bedroom, nursery, kitchen, and bath; these would incorporate more space than the entire existing building. Paul Bierman-Lytle decided to leave the existing space unaltered (with the exception of cathedralizing the ceiling to relieve the spatial squeeze) and add on

DESIGNER'S STATEMENT

The original building was used as a library for its owner, a judge. The interior consisted of wainscoting around the entire perimeter, serving as a base for floor-to-ceiling bookshelves. The floor was wide planks of pine; the fieldstone fireplace was set into the wood paneling.

Typical of New England houses, the siding was white clapboard with semicircular Palladian attic windows, large wood doors, and stone chimneys.

The building is located on estate grounds bounded by fieldstone walls, expansive lawns, vegetable gardens, and apple and pear trees and in view of tidal inlets and marshes.

The addition was designed to be sensitive to these surroundings and remain in the character of the neighboring estate buildings. Due to budget and time constraints, the project was developed into two phases of expansion. Phase I consisted of extending the house in a mirrored image of itself, creating a pedestal where the final addition of second and third floors would complete roof lines and strengthen the symmetry, again a characteristic of early traditional homes. —*Paul Bierman-Lytle*

all those elements that turn a lodge into a house.

The trick came in seeing the symmetry possible by replicating asymmetry, mirroring the form of the existing structure and creating a joining piece. Using the kitchen as the connecting crux of the mirrored extension of Phase I, the architect created a formal link indicating the appropriate functional connection between the living and sleeping zones of the house.

This first step keyed the ultimate form of the project. Since materials, geometries, and forms would be mirrored, the second phase of the scheme would simply launch off the first vertically, using the existing roof pitches to create a new master bedroom and bath and leaving the bedroom and nursery downstairs created by Phase I for the post-infancy children.

The result is perhaps the most literal and whimsical interpretation of generative Contextualism possible given the enormous transition of box to house. An economical double utilization of all structural and mechanical addenda realized in Phase I can be seen in Phase II.

Perhaps because Paul Bierman-Lytle was so thoroughly empowered by his designer-builder-client status, his freedom of formal invention was unburdened by such a modest parent building.

fig. 1 *Original material. This rustic outbuilding housed paneling salvaged by the original estate owner around the turn of the century.*

fig. 2 *Phase I. The mirrored mass to the left houses the master bedroom, child's bedroom, and bath; the connector is the kitchen and mudroom.*

fig. 3 *Phase II (unrealized as yet). A second-floor living room rests atop the kitchen with an even loftier master bedroom at the peak of the extended roof plane. The living and dining area in the original building is transformed into a dining room, while the two bedrooms of the Phase I addition are transformed into a children's wing.*

*Line drawings by the architect
Photos by Joan Sussman*

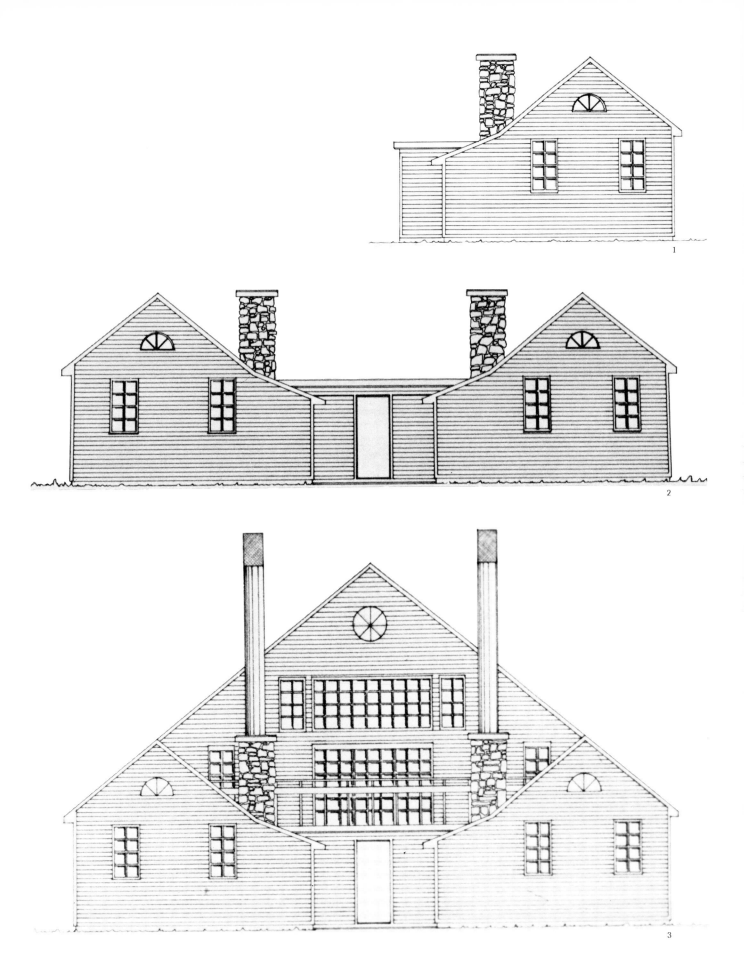

1

2

3

4

fig. 4 *South side. The existing library in the foreground generates the new addition to the west. Note that the temporary chrome flue in the connector awaits the masonry chimney of Phase II.*

fig. 5 *North side. The kitchen connector breaks to accommodate the tree grid of the orchard.*

fig. 6 *Connector interior. Simple laminate kitchen stays low to mitigate the pinch of its small space. Cabinets in left background serve as a latter-day exposed pantry.*

5

6

A Two-Faced Approach

Mark McInturff revives a derelict and celebrates the rescue of a house in suburban Washington, D.C.

PROJECT PROFILE

McInturff residence
Location: Bethesda, Md.
Architect: Mark McInturff,
Wiebenson & McInturff, Architects
Budget: $40,000
Area renovated: 1000 ft^2
Area added: 300 ft^2

Shrouded in asphaltic brick shingle siding, a decaying 1200-square-foot house stood upon the edge of a hill overlooking the Potomac River. The tenuous quality of the siting was reinforced by the obvious sense of degenerative structural rot and general disrepair. Not surprisingly, when the house plus a parcel of land became available, its physical condition did not engender an enthusiastic response from potential buyers.

A low, low price and the clear promise of such a wild lot in a dense suburban situation forced Catherine and Mark McInturff to give in to their quixotic leanings. Once the house was purchased, the immediate need to let a lean-to addition die a merciful death was met, and over the next three years Mark McInturff regenerated this modest box and brought forth a most positive realization of rebirth.

Only the northern wall was salvaged; the rest of the existing frame of the house was either replaced or renovated beyond the point of recognition. Rather than remake a new building in his own image, the owner-

OWNER-ARCHITECT'S STATEMENT

This house is important to me for several reasons. First, it is the product of my own labor, including all demolition; carpentry, concrete, Sheetrock, and trim work; and painting. No part of the original house remains unaltered. Before construction began, the center of the house was caving in, the roof leaked, and the exterior was covered with asphaltic brick siding (fortunately covering good wood siding that was matched in the new work). Part of the house had to be demolished. The rest was restructured, and all systems were replaced. Doing the work myself on weekends, evenings, and vacations over a three-year period allowed me the time to develop the design slowly, revising it during construction. Such luxury of time is rarely available for a client, nor is there usually an opportunity to use a house as a testing ground for ideas and methods.
—*Mark McInturff*

architect based his design on the latent memory of the original hillside cottage.

The street facade was renovated but left essentially unchanged—simple and semi-symmetrical. That symmetry softly explodes on the private, river-facing facade.

The design is based on a simple cross axis of a central column arcade that replaced a bearing wall on the long axis and the existing bisecting central stair dividing living and eating areas on the first floor and bedrooms above. The play of space and light around and about these ordering elements evidences a lyric expression quietly spawned by the archaic form facing the street.

The exterior has but a single siding material, painted clapboards, and all roofing is asphalt shingles. Windows and angular geometries express the released energy of the hillside facade. In keeping the methods of his expression simple and by basing his spatial and formal frolics on the most familiar of house forms, Mark McInturff spans the broad gap of time between the original derelict and his present delight.

1

fig. 1 *Side view. An orderly progression of clapboard lines and eave heights gives the promise of an impending event. Note the new concrete piers supporting the new addition, which replaced the lean-to at the outset of the project.*

fig. 2 *Site axonometric. House described at left corner. New house under construction is at center of image.*

Photos and line drawings by the architect

2

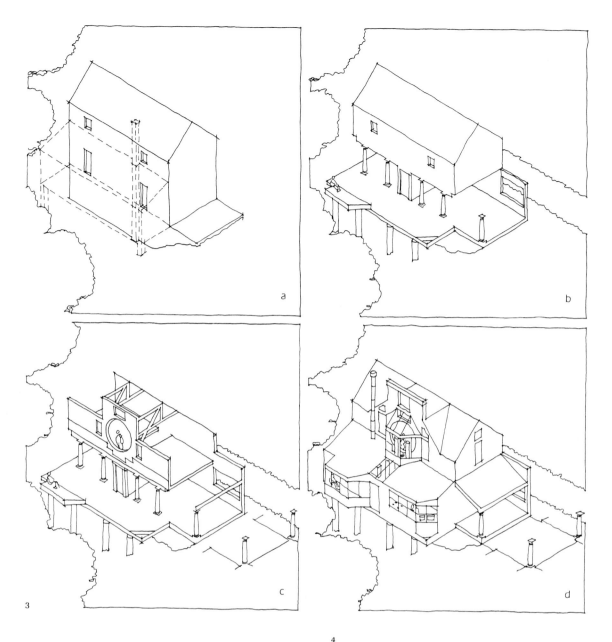

a

b

c

3

d

4

fig. 3 *Construction sequence. (a) original lean-to addition removed, (b) new first-floor deck extended on new concrete piers, colonnade replaces existing wall, (c) new interior elevation at second floor faces the river, and (d) house fully enclosed.*

fig. 4 *Front view. A restored farmhouse tight to the street.*

5

fig. 5 *Perhaps naval in origin, the billowing extensions toward a river view somehow simultaneously point the way to the view and beckon the observer to come inside.*

fig. 6 *Plans for the first and second floors. The axes of stair and colonnade provide a datum for the development of the river-view facade. This is a minimum-sized family dwelling, with but one bath, two bedrooms, and basic spatial separations.*

6

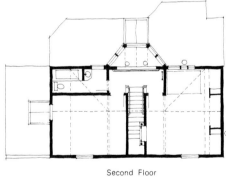

Second Floor

First Floor

0   5   10

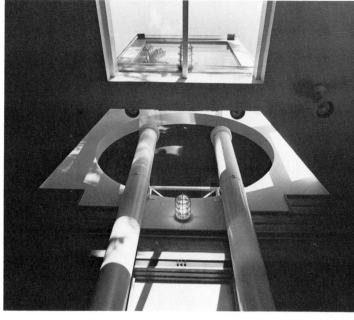

fig. 7   Living room. A wood stove serves to center the space. Note the discontinuity of the beam before it touches the wall at right. In keeping with this desire for building parts to announce themselves, ceiling joists are exposed as is the gypsum-wallboard edge. Perhaps a testament to the complete rebuilding by the owner-architect, the primary result is an informal sense of casual architectural exhibitionism.

fig. 8   The vertical event connecting the two floors and the intersection of the stair and colonnade axes. Industrial lighting fixtures and overtly attached ornamental columns reinforce the sense of "pieces and parts" architecture.

fig. 9   Interior colonnade. This is a new axial ordinate defining the back of the house and generating the ceiling break that allows for further vertical perforation of the ceiling plane at the head of the stairs (center top of picture). The typically exterior detailing brought indoors signals a change in scale and orientation and draws attention to the applied nature of the space facing the river view.

fig. 10   Head of the stairs. This is the lone circular element in the entire house, which signals the spiritual heart of the house. The disintegral quality of the detailing tends to create an antigravitational feeling of formal and physical release.

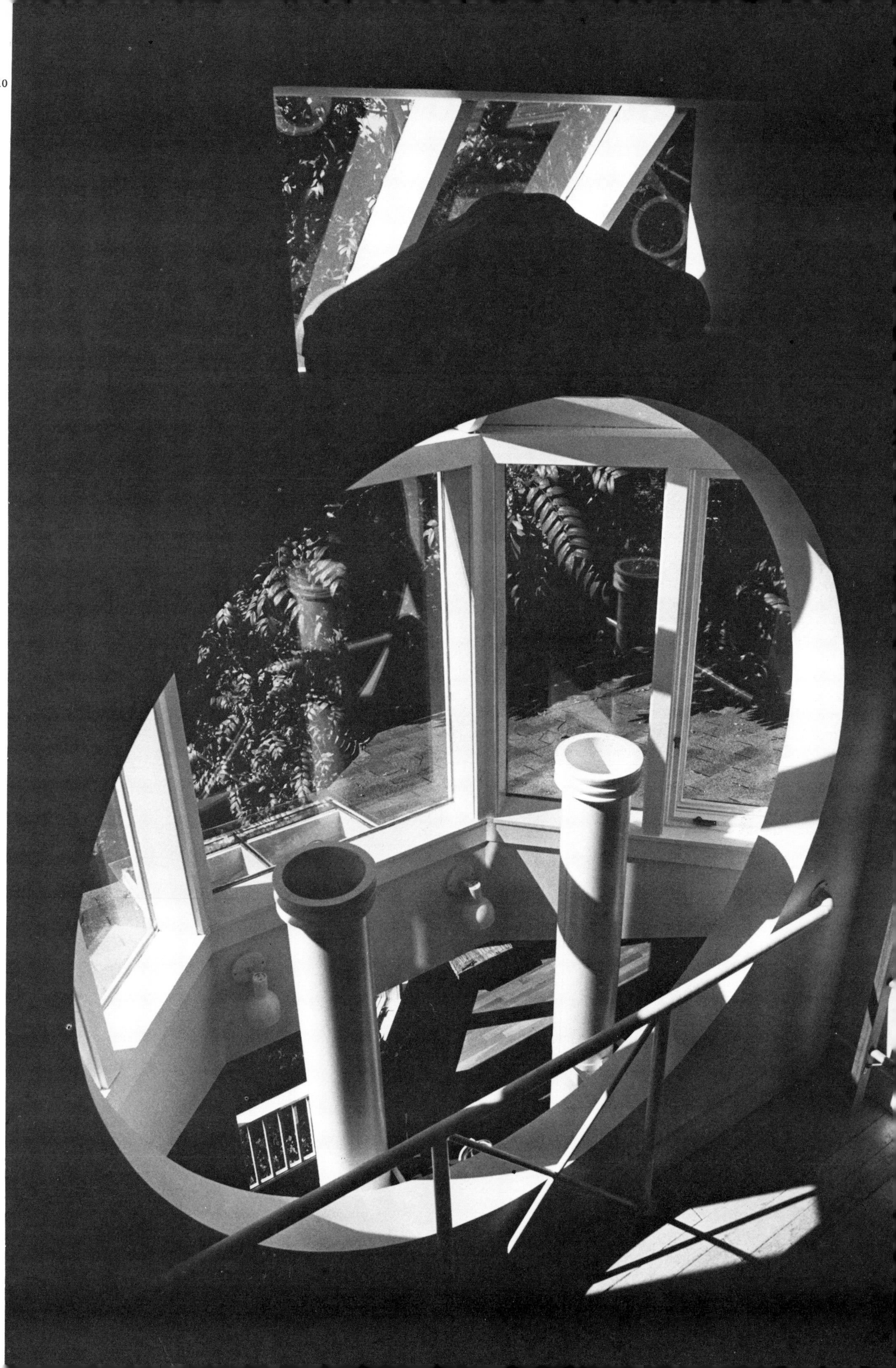

Reaching Toward Heaven

*Bart Prince creates an expressive masterpiece
from an expressionless house in California.*

The home of Margo and Dale Seymour was a study in the connected-shed style of building in rural California. The massing appeared to be boxes running into each other, with the ensemble arranged to avoid trees and the expense of basements or second stories.

Rarely has so little spawned so much.

A couple with less vision would have hired a builder to fix the sagging wall, resurface the rotting siding, and add yet another shack to the rambling array. Even if the couple had opted to take their desires and needs to an architect, the normal reaction of most designers might be to reject all but the best parts of the existing building and perhaps extend some quietly distinctive box from the remaining structure.

But fortunately a thoroughly ordinary building had the benefit of owners who found an extraordinary architect, Bart Prince. Prince turned a blind eye toward the obvious mundanity and pulled out almost all the conceptual stops to create a realized fantasy. More than any other project in this book, the Seymour addition stretches the limits of architectural form when melded with an existing structure. By retaining the existing bland building's extremities and focusing on the central portion of the house, Prince creates the sense of an aesthetic explosion amidst the tepid sea of bland building.

In short, a new kitchen, hot tub, sauna, family room, master bedroom, and decks were added, creating the California home proper where once only simple accommodation existed.

The only—and most crucial—carryover

PROJECT PROFILE

Seymour residence
Location: Los Altos, Calif.
Architect: Bart Prince
Budget: $150,000
Area renovated: 700 ft²
Area added: 700 ft²

OWNERS' STATEMENT

We *had* to do something about our house (one wall was bowing strangely), and we wanted to do something drastic, something different and artistic. We thought that no good architect would want to bother with a remodel. We also felt that architects were for rich, important people not for us.

Yet we had this lovely site. We got caught up in Bart's vision of what could emerge from our somber cocoon. We gambled on his very untraditional design.

And we are glad we did. Have we sacrificed for the design? A little function? Time? Money? Probably. But sometimes the way the sun and shapes interact makes us shiver with the beauty. We're lucky to be living in this wondrous piece of sculpture.
—*Margo and Dale Seymour*

ARCHITECT'S STATEMENT

My general feeling about design is that there should be a creative and unique approach to each problem.

The clients' needs or demands were not extraordinary. The project is only different in the way it addresses the problems. So many architects say to me, "I wish I had clients like that," when in fact they do!

In this project the existing home is something you see all the time—a cabin in the woods, not so much designed as just plain built. If there's nothing there to start with, then one is given great license.—*Bart Prince*

from the remaining house to the new addition is the use of traditional redwood shingles, but once the addition begins to grow out of the existing structure, the shingles become thoroughly animated in pattern and wall shape. Without this integration, the addition might appear as a predator consuming a passive victim, rather than an organic extension of the existing house.

All other materials other than the siding are new. Laminated wood beams, concrete walls and piers, plexiglas glazing, and steel columns and bracing all are brought into play to create a wholly new entity bounded by the familiar bookend building remnants. Similarly, the new spaces are without discernible limit or precedent in the given context.

It has been said that there are no straight lines in nature, and this addition is expressive of the most organic of aesthetic intentions. The shingle skin billows with the ripe fullness of a well-watered tropical plant.

In facing the large Plexiglas-glazed areas north, the architect responded to views down the existing site's slope and prevented unwanted overheating in the warm climate of southern California. In creating a tall central space to vent hot air and a masonry mass at its core to serve as a thermal flywheel, Prince allowed for passive cooling of the entire house.

A lot of words might attempt to reconcile the spirit of this addition to the conscious mind of the reader, but this is one project where words serve only to blunt the power expressed in the visual images shown.

fig. 1 *An exuberant dialogue between the various parts, existing, new, and natural. The new house in the lower right launches a new roof extension into the new north-facing addition. The tree seems to intertwine with the form as the roof reaches to touch it. Redwood shingle patterns flow with the implicit energy of the addition's organic form. Note the Plexiglass clerestory glazing above the lower window wall opening up into a deck.*

Photos and line drawings by the architect

2

3

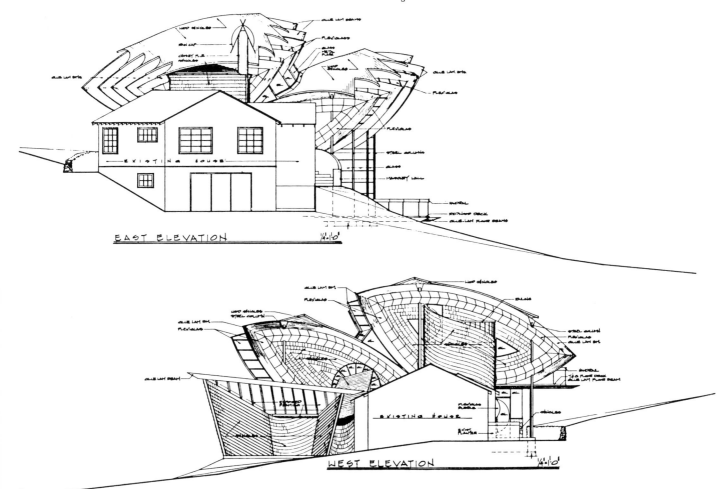

EAST ELEVATION   ¼"=1'0"

WEST ELEVATION   ¼"=1'0"

4

5

fig. 2 *View from the north. The radially organized laminated beams ascend from left to right. Note the direct expression of laminated wood beams, steel columns, and infilling fenestration, all in the lush embrace of the surrounding woods.*

fig. 3 *Note the clear contrasts of the original traditional building (left), curving clerestory glazing and roof structure (upper right), and the diagonal window wall at ground level.*

fig. 4 *Elevations. Because of the dense forest and varied terrain, these drawings offer the best clue of the architect's approach. Existing buildings serve as remnant bookends to a hyperkinetic explosion of spiritual expression amidships (as it were).*

fig. 5 *Family room deck. The sweep of the double laminated beams is articulated by infill glazing that frames the shingle panel (upper left). Amid the formal fullness, the steel columns present a stark support and define the corners for the window wall at ground level. Note the radiating decking reaching out to the pedestrian. Similarly animated, the retaining wall in the foreground has its own life amid the concert of shapes and materials.*

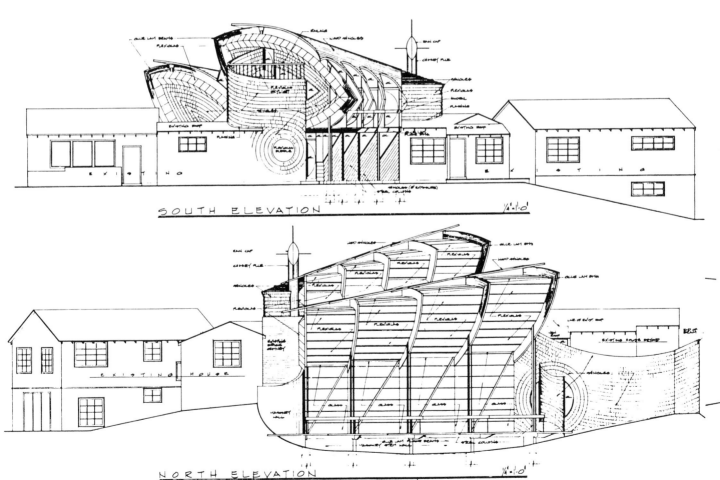

SOUTH ELEVATION

NORTH ELEVATION

6

fig. 6 *View from the west. The master bedroom bath expresses its back as an emerging hemicycle form, shrouded in flowing laminations of redwood shingles. The meager original building can be seen to the left, with a new surfacing of shingles—a skin that becomes more uncontrolled as it encounters the new portion of the building. The house's back door can be seen to the lower right. Note how windows are either ignored or embraced by the flow of the shingling pattern.*

fig. 7 *South wall, as seen from the east. The back bones extend from beneath their skin, and an elevated deck serving the master bedroom dissociates this part of the addition from the ground. Note the existing roof to the lower right.*

fig. 8 *South wall. This view of the new construction from the center point of the beam's radial pattern affords an open view through the entire addition. The roof seems to be lightly resting on the dynamic beaming.*

7

8

9

fig. 9 *View of entry. Inside the organism, the skeleton becomes even more explicit and the trapped space can harbor the overtly sculptural entry terminus, a shingled shrouded chute encountering a medallion of shingles. Note the steel bracing and columns and diffusing clerestory Plexiglas glazing.*

fig. 10 *View from the east. From the humble shed a miraculous effervescence of form and structure rises to the light. Note that the redwood shingle roof of the existing remnant shed becomes a bulging, taut skin stretched over the exposed laminated "bones" of the new addition.*

fig. 11 *(opposite) Entry view. In the formal entry, one encounters a symbolic patch of wall surrounded by a radial pattern of glazing muntins and an arcing beam emerging from the concrete walls of the family room as a stair beckons. Stringy steel, infill glazing, billowing walls, monolithic concrete, and effluently dynamic shingling create a harmony of explicit differentiation. Soaring structure is bathed in light and space with a freedom of spirit that defies explicit definition. Note the consistent use of materials both inside and out, which reinforces a given element's identity and serves to create a clarity that can accept the radical expressionist treatment.*

10

Connecticut Kinetics

*Roderic M. Hartung takes the complex
requirements of a couple
approaching retirement and creates
a rich ensemble of forms and spaces.*

When Robert and Marcella Congdon found the future site for their retirement home, it had more history than utility. Two simple buildings sat on the small parcel of land in the prototypically New England town of Old Lyme, Connecticut. One had been the schoolhouse for the town, the other an old barn; both had been relocated and renovated by a local hero, Senator Tommy Ball, in the early years of the twentieth century.

As years advanced, the Congdons, based in New Jersey, had the time, distance, and inclination to come up with a list of desirable changes that would facilitate the conversion of two vacation cottages into a full-time retirement home.

It's best to let Marcella Congdon's words convey the high points of this list.

My husband and I dreamed of connecting the two buildings, having a large "Keeping Room," a life-size kitchen, and first floor master bed-dressing-sitting room suite with a guest room and bath in an upstairs where one could stand up. As a retirement home, doorways should be wide enough for wheelchairs, there should be no extraneous steps, and exterior entries lend themselves to the eventual ramp; we had seen far too many elderly relatives become captive to their houses. As the oil crisis was on, we wanted efficiency, conservation of heat, and many south-facing windows. Our Norwich Terriers would live with us in part of the house but other parts would be dog-free for our allergic two-legged friends. A tiny yard and close neighbors would require an interesting facade on all four sides, and the showpiece gray beech made the arrangement of the lot a great challenge.

Rod Hartung took this list plus zoning and site-access requirements (due to restricted road frontage) and saw the opportunities yet present in the restrictions imposed.

First of all, space had to be added. It was obvious that a linking building would not only add new space but create one large home where two distinct forms once sat in-

OWNER'S STATEMENT

Our great good fortune was to find an architect who saw all this as a challenge and who funneled his great creative energies into the design. We are delighted with the result. The "new" house is functional and energy-efficient, but more, it is a dynamic work of art. I think even if we become deaf, dumb, and blind, we can *live* in this friendly and stimulating house. —*Marcella H. Congdon*

ARCHITECT'S STATEMENT

Although the architectural style of the neighborhood is basically Colonial, this early New England town kept up to date with the architectural periods that came along, and thus a sprinkling of Federal, Greek revival, Italianate, and, later, Victorian elements caused a heterogeneous blend of different architectural styles. The design chosen would use certain Colonial and Classical elements to give it dignity and assure its compatibility with its neighbors, but it would be innovative and not strive to be an authentic reproduction or restoration.—*Roderic M. Hartung*

communicado. Rather than opt for an expedient link between the existing structures, Hartung saw the potential in moving those simple buildings in the manner of the renovating Senator Ball some seventy years ago.

The Congdons wanted the beauty and utility of a great Keeping Room, or very large, open living room. Hartung responded by gutting the existing barn interior and moving its structure to the southeast corner of the site, separating its lovely spatial volume from the prosaic garage function tacked on by the good senator. Having allowed for the distinct formal expression of the barn cum Keeping Room from the garage (whose location is fixed due to the restricted road frontage mentioned above), Hartung created an entry courtyard between the three basic buildings. Showing a further willingness to recreate an ensemble by revitalizing the existing pieces, Hartung recycled the existing barn door as the entry to the courtyard, and hence to the house.

To link the Keeping Room with the schoolhouse-cum-bedroom wing, Hartung created a connector that demurred to the two existing buildings it joined. As a single-story, greenhoused-glazed form, it expressed a contemporary presence in a small sea of New England shapes and materials.

To further create a house for the 1980s from eighteenth-century components, Hartung raised the hip of the schoolhouse roof to accommodate a second floor for guest bedroom space. It's important to recognize the sympathy evidenced by the architect for the form he dealt with. It would have been easier to simply raise the roof to allow a habitable second floor, but Hartung recognized the importance of scale in creating his courtyard and presenting a house to the street by maintaining the eave height and then adding four dormers to attain sufficient headroom for occupancy.

Melanie Grimes

fig. 1 *New entry. Under the watchful eye of a new dormer added to accommodate a bath is the existing schoolhouse building. The existing barn entry doors were relocated onto an appropriately blank, vertically sided wall. Lattice panels allow a friendly visual penetration into the awaiting courtyard. By introducing a distinctively expressive curving corniced wall backdrop to this icon of entry, the architect provided a lightly symbolic indication of the old being reused in a new context.*

figs. 2 & 3 *Before and after axonometric drawings. These drawings clearly show the reorientation of the existing barn, the reuse of the existing barn entry, the addition of the kitchen connector, and the new bedroom dormers on the schoolhouse building. Note the removed shed addition to the barn and the completely new garage built in the location mandated by the limited-access requirement. Note also the crucial location of the gray beech tree (indicated as a truncated object) in the foreground as well as the development of exterior spaces surrounding the newly agglomerated form.*

Line drawings by the architect

1

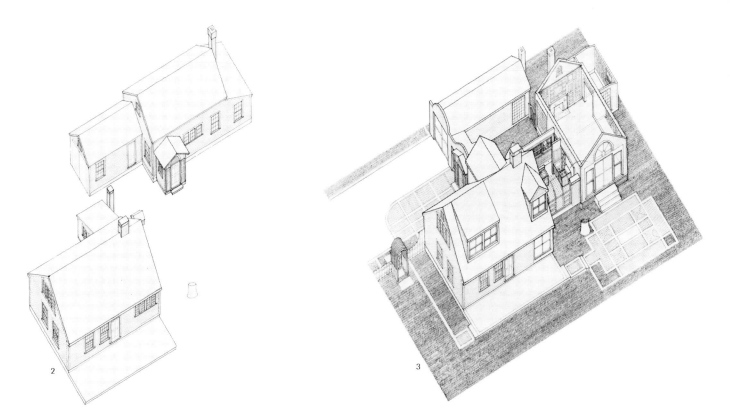

2

3

STORAGE STOR

GUEST EXER

dn

UPPER LEVEL

fig. 4 *Lower-level (bottom) and upper-level plans. In these drawings the walls drawn with thick black lines are new construction and the walls drawn with double lines are existing construction. An entry courtyard was realized by moving the existing barn and building a new garage-shop and a kitchen between the existing buildings. The new master bedroom suite now occupies the entire first floor of the existing schoolhouse, allowing a single-floor use pattern essential for a retirement home.*

fig. 5 *Transitional gable, interior view. Located at the juncture of the old schoolhouse to the left and the new kitchen to the right, the gable exposes the existing post-and-beam construction. Note the new oak ceiling paneling.*

fig. 6 *New dormers on the schoolhouse roof. Marvelously expressive of where new meets old, the new kitchen roof eave (left) springs the transitional gable onto the mass of the existing schoolhouse, thus resolving a potentially awkward intersection. Depending on the perspective, the new bath dormer to the right either acts as the mother to or is the rational extension of the aforementioned gable. With the use of custom, fixed, curved windows for both gables, three distinct features are realized. First, the gables are connected by the similar window motifs. Second, the custom, anticatalog quality of the windows enhances the sense of New England craftsmanship present in the existing buildings. And last, with the introduction of curves into a rectilinear system of glazing, the new gables quietly assert their independence.*

fig. 7 *Courtyard entry. Looking through the new window on the north end of the Keeping Room, one can see the new entry.*

GARAGE SHOP

STUDY

COURTYARD

GALLERY

FOYER

CLOS

KIT

HALL

BR

4

LOWER LEVEL

5

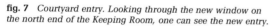

Roderic M. Hartung

6

7   Jeremy Dodd

Perhaps it is the nature of these dormers that best ex-emplifies an enlightened vision of adding onto an existing form. The four gables dare to be different and yet are a coherent group. One dormer serves to harbor a bath, one a bedroom, another to get light into a corridor. The last dor-mer serves to express the connection of the new kitchen to the existing schoolhouse on the exterior, and on the interior it allows the schoolhouse post-and-beam structure to be bared at the point of entry. By making each dormer distinct in form, Hartung achieves a whimsical, almost ad hoc massing, creating a delightful variation of scale and move-ment. All of this is achieved while providing the most es-sential of physical requirements—human accommodation.

Rod Hartung took on the task of total remodeling without violent change. His new realization seems merely to ani-mate and express the latent forms he started with. By re-siding the entire complex in consistently spaced clap-boards, the architect has given the new variations a coherent basis for existing. It is this sense of natural progression and organic growth that creates such a happy marriage of antique forms and contemporary utility.

fig. 8 *Keeping Room, north wall. By fortunate accident, oak paneling was discovered during the gutting of the barn and was restored to surround a new Italian verd antique marble fireplace front*

fig. 9 *Entry corridor and kitchen, as seen from the Keeping Room. Serving as both a link between the two older buildings and as its own space, the new kitchen-entry is appropriately framed as a subspace to the grand Keeping Room. Note that the kitchen can be made completely separate from the larger space by use of a sliding door and movable panels.*

8

9

10

11

fig. 10 *Southern elevation. Virtually all the glazing shown is new; note the variety of scale in pane size and the simple expression of the different building parts by the means of varying window types.*

fig. 11 *Keeping Room, south wall. Passive solar heat gain is created by the new glazing shown, and the vista presented is protected by the large existing trees yet opens the space to the world outside.*

ARCHITECTS' AND DESIGNERS' DIRECTORY

Leon Armantrout, Day & Armantrout, P.O. Box 1006, 409 Orange Street, Redlands, California 92373

Paul Bierman-Lytle, P.O. Box 239, Guilford, Connecticut 06437

Kent Bloomer, Leetes Island Road, Guilford, Connecticut 06437

Bohlin/Powell/Larkin/Cywinski, Wilkes-Barre/Pittsburgh/Philadelphia

Turner Brooks and Stuart Hamilton, Starksboro, Vermont 05487

BumpZoid, 260 Fifth Avenue, New York, New York 10001

Arne Bystrom, 1617 Post Alley, Seattle, Washington 98101

Wm. T. Cannady & Associates, Inc., P.O. Box 25377, Houston, Texas 77005

Cass & Pinnell, 1532 Sixteenth Street NW, Washington, D.C. 20036

Fernau/Hartman, 1555 La Vereda, Berkeley, California 94708

Chad Floyd, Moore Grover Harper, Essex, Connecticut 06426

Graham Gund, 12 Arrow Street, Cambridge, Massachusetts 02178

Roderic M. Hartung, 77 Main Street, Essex, Connecticut 06426

Mark Isaacs, Energy-Efficient Architectural Design, Rogers Street Fire House, 1122 Rogers Street, Louisville, Kentucky 40204

Jersey Devil, Box 145, Stockton, New Jersey 08559

Martin Henry Kaplan, 107 South Main #208, Seattle, Washington 98104

Leung Hemmler Camayd, 428 Spruce Street, Scranton, Pennsylvania 18503

Donlyn Lyndon, Lyndon/Buchanan Associates, 946 Parker Street, Berkeley, California 94710

Mark McInturff, Wiebenson & McInturff, Architects, 1734 Connecticut Avenue NW, Washington, D.C. 20009

Louis Mackall & Partner (Duo Dickinson), 50 Maple Street, Branford, Connecticut 06405

Bart Prince, 813 Carlislene, Albuquerque, New Mexico 87106

Eric K. Rekdahl, Rekdahl Tellefsen Associates, 819 Ensenada, Berkeley, California 94703

Shope Reno Wharton Associates, 18 West Putnam, Greenwich, Connecticut 06830

William F. Stern, 4902 Travis Street, Houston, Texas 77002

Harry Teague, Box 4684, Aspen, Colorado 81611

Susana Torre, The Architecture Studio, 242 West Thirty-eighth Street, New York, New York 10018

Zar & Hicks, 914 West Carman, Chicago, Illinois 60607

INDEX

ABOUT THE AUTHOR

Duo Dickinson, a registered architect, is the partner of Louis Mackall & Partner, Architects, a team that has designed over twenty additions in the past five years.

His practice has concentrated on residential design, particularly on innovative approaches to renovating and adding onto buildings. He has also served as a designer for Breakfast Woodworks, one of the finest millwork houses in the eastern region of the country. He is a graduate of Cornell University's College of Architecture, Art and Planning.